PRAISE FOR THE AUTHOR

"Danny and his team bring a high level of insight, knowledge, and integrity to the online business world."

-Guy Kawasaki, Chief evangelist of Canva
and author of The Art of the Start 2.0

"I've been consistently impressed with Danny; not just how smart he is, but also how giving he is with his expertise and generous spirit."

-Brian Kurtz, founder of Titans Marketing LLC,
formerly of Boardroom Inc.

"Danny and his team are a model of professionalism and quality. Anyone who's serious about online marketing should be following what they're doing."

-Michael Port, New York Times
best-selling author of Steal the Show

"Danny Iny and his organization are an utterly thorough and high-quality team of people delivering excellent products. I love sending people to Danny and team because I know they're in good hands and will come out the other end super smart and ready to tackle the world."

-Chris Brogan, CEO Owner Media Group

ONLINE COURSES

A BUSINESS PARABLE...

About Creating Freedom by
Teaching Your Gift

Danny Iny

MIRASEE PRESS

5750 Avenue Notre Dame de Grace
Montreal, Quebec
H4A 1M4, Canada
www.mirasee.com

Paperback ISBN: 978-1-7347725-8-6
Hardback ISBN: 978-1-7347725-9-3
E-book ISBN: 978-1-7347725-7-9

1 3 5 7 9 10 8 6 4 2

This book is dedicated to my family.
Thank you for reminding me every day of what really matters.

Download the Audiobook + Online Course Business Bundle!

READ THIS FIRST

Just to say thank you for reading my book, I'd love to share the audiobook version (narrated by a team of actors!) PLUS the audio versions of two other books I've written about online course businesses: *Teach Your Gift,* and *Effortless*.

—Danny Iny

Go to **OnlineCourses.Rocks/bundle** to get it!

Contents

Preface   I

Chapter 1: Crash!   1

Chapter 2: Amy's Dad   7

Chapter 3: Mastermind   13

Chapter 4: Amy's 'Little' Formula   21

Chapter 5: Dinner   27

Chapter 6: The Baby Manual   35

Chapter 7: Running   37

Chapter 8: Back to the Mastermind   41

Chapter 9: Coming Clean   49

Chapter 10: The Challenge   51

Chapter 11: Asking for Help   57

Chapter 12: Getting Serious   61

Chapter 13: Game Plan   69

Chapter 14: Rick   75

Chapter 15: Results   79

Chapter 16: Pilot   85

Chapter 17: Sleepless   95

Chapter 18: Locked Out   101

Chapter 19: Selling   103

Chapter 20: Last Day   109

Epilogue: Doing Stuff That Matters   115

Teach Your Gift   121

About the Author   137

PREFACE

I n the summer of 2020, like much of the world facing the COVID-19 pandemic, my family and I were under lockdown. With two small children, we binged our way through the entire catalog of Disney classics. We got stuck repeating a few titles over and over again (*Sleeping Beauty* and *Cinderella* were particularly popular with our kids), rediscovered some long-forgotten gems (like *101 Dalmatians* and *The Sword in the Stone*), and were disappointed to see that some old favorites hadn't aged well (the depiction of Native Americans in *Peter Pan* is strikingly racist, and *Pinocchio* is just really creepy!). Each movie led to its own imaginary games; my kids spent more hours than I can count dressed as this or that princess, and perfecting the art of 'accidentally' losing a slipper while coming down the stairs.

After watching *Mulan* there was all the jumping and punching and kicking that you might expect, but the movie seemed to make a stronger-than-usual impression. That night, when I put my daughter to bed, she told me that she wants to learn karate.

This was music to my ears. I had discovered martial arts as a teenager, and spent the better part of a decade training and teaching (I was always a much better teacher than practitioner). In my training I had found confidence, discipline, and a philosophy towards facing and overcoming adversity – all things that I was eager to share with my daughter. So I bought her a *gi*, and started mulling over lesson plans. Now, back in my training days I had learned by heart the entire 233 technique syllabus from white to brown belt... so imagine my surprise when I realized that other than little bits and pieces, I couldn't remember any of it!

Of course, it's like riding a bike – once I got back into it, it started coming back pretty quickly. But still, I was surprised at how much had slipped my mind, given the thousands upon thousands of hours that I had spent practicing and teaching this stuff.

Now, right around the same time I was re-watching the first two seasons of the *Karate Kid* television sequel *Cobra Kai*, in anticipation of the forthcoming third season. It was striking how I noticed all the easter eggs, and remembered every bit of dialog from movies that I hadn't seen in years! Which I'm sure tracks with your own experience; odds are that I can bring to your mind the entirety of Daniel Larusso's karate education with just four words: "wax on, wax off". That's enough for you to remember the chores of washing and waxing cars, sanding floors, and painting fences as a stealth way of practicing blocking motions, leading to the scene where it all comes to a head: Daniel Larusso is frustrated with all the work and about to quit on the whole process, when Mr. Miyagi surprises him with a flurry of punches and kicks that Daniel blocks through sheer force of muscle memory.

Now, why is it that I can remember the intricacies of a fake training process that I never participated in (thankfully, since it wouldn't actually work!) better than a real training routine that I performed for literally thousands of hours? Simple: our brains aren't wired to remember *routines*, but they are wired to embrace and retain *stories*. Story is the best tool at our disposal for grabbing and holding attention, and for creating a desire to know what happens next. I mean, was there ever a class or lecture that you looked forward to as much as the release of *Avengers: Endgame*?! If so, I'd sure like to meet the professor who managed that trick, and learn their secrets!

This isn't to say that facts and information can't be interesting – of course they can. But the teacher does have to work a lot harder to make them as interesting as a story naturally is. And, when they manage to do it, it's usually because they ended up leaning on stories as a tool to get the job done. Case in point are the overwhelmingly successful works of authors like Malcolm Gladwell, Adam Grant, and Chip and Dan Heath – they're all brimming with stories.

I've learned from their examples and leaned on stories in my own writing, including in multiple books on the topic of online courses. But there's a difference between a book that teaches facts with the assistance of stories, and a book that *tells* a story to help the reader understand important facts. Done well, the latter is dramatically more powerful. For example, it would be very hard to write a book about managing supply chains more engaging than Eliyahu Goldratt's classic *The Goal*, and even though my shelves are filled with books about leadership, none are as accessible and fun to read as Patrick Lencioni's leadership fables (like *Five Dysfunctions of a Team*, *Three Signs of a Miserable Job*, and *Death by Meeting*).

In this book, I've done my best to follow those examples of taking a topic important enough to warrant struggling to master it, and make it accessible, relatable, and engaging enough that the learning is a treat rather than a chore. Through the story of Amy Morgan, you will get a front-row seat to the experiences and challenges faced by coaches, consultants, speakers, authors, and experts as they work to build their online course businesses. You'll learn the things that they have to figure out (often the hard way!) to make it work, and you'll hopefully enjoy being along for the ride.

Now we're almost ready to dive in, but first there's one thing that I'd be remiss not to mention. Everyone reading these words knows that we live in exceptional, unusual times. In the last year and a half the world has been turned upside down, shaken hard, and turned upside down again. We've faced wave upon wave of a global pandemic, along with the economic fallout from the shutdowns meant to contain its spread. The murder of George Floyd was the match that ignited the too-long-ignored powder keg of racial injustice in the United States and around the world. We've seen unprecedented environmental upheaval in the form of hurricanes, floods, and wildfires, to the point where it wouldn't be an exaggeration to say that much of the world has been aflame. And of course, there has been the widening political polarization that came with the American elections, culminating in literal insurrection at the nation's capital. So to say that we live in crazy times would be an enormous understatement!

These crazy times have been a big part of what prompted me to write this book. Not because I wanted to reflect these many upheavals in the narrative –you won't find mentions of pandemics, face masks, or social distancing in this story, nor will you find any mention of environmental challenges, political divides, or racial injustice (though I have done my best to portray in the story the real diversity of backgrounds and perspectives that inform our everyday lives, and the experiences of real everyday entrepreneurs). But this book is informed by the times in which we live, because both the need and opportunity for online course entrepreneurs have been dramatically accelerated by all these events. That's why the online course industry is experiencing more growth than it has seen since its inception decades ago, and why smart entrepreneurs are jumping to seize this opportunity.

I hope you will be one of them, and that this book will serve as both a nudge and a guide to support you in your efforts to create leverage, freedom, and impact by teaching your gift.

P.S. You do NOT need to read this entire book before also taking some next steps to connect with me and with my company Mirasee's course building and marketing training. Feel free to take advantage of the invitations on the next page NOW.

Bonus resources to support you!

GET THE ONLINE COURSE BUSINESS BUNDLE (FREE)

The audiobook version of this book (narrated by a team of actors!) PLUS the audio versions of two other books I've written about online course businesses: Teach Your Gift, and Effortless..

→ Download it at **OnlineCourses.Rocks/bundle**

PARTICIPATE IN THE COURSE BUILDER'S BOOTCAMP (FREE)

Ready to start your own online course business journey? Our weeklong intensive Course Builder's Bootcamp is a crash course in everything you need to get started.

→ Sign up for free at **OnlineCourses.Rocks/bootcamp**

JOIN US IN PERSON AT TEACH YOUR GIFT LIVE

Receive best-in-class training, discover cutting-edge strategies, and connect with a community of your fellow coach, consultant, author, speaker, and expert entrepreneurs.

→ Reserve your spot at **OnlineCourses.Rocks/live**

Chapter 1
CRASH!

Amy Morgan slowly cruised the packed parking lot of the Pacific Heights shopping center. As she looked for a parking spot, her thoughts drifted back to the previous night.

Well, that was a bust! I can't believe I missed dinner with the kids for that.

Amy had been exploring different entrepreneurial opportunities for months – reading articles, watching videos, and attending webinars at inconveniently scheduled times. She knew that last night's topic was a long shot for her, but she was resolved to try everything until she found a path that felt right. The webinar had been about flipping houses; finding what the presenter called "distressed real-estate" – which basically means the owners were in a real jam – and buying it cheap. Then turning around and selling it, presumably at a higher price.

How is that supposed to work, anyway? I mean, if the person selling it to me can't find someone who'll pay a higher price, why would I be able to?

The training had claimed that there were techniques for finding those more lucrative buyers, but never got around to sharing what those techniques actually were. For that, you had to join their "inner circle" training program. It was supposedly for people just starting out, but the price tag made Amy wonder.

$10,000 just to learn how to do this? And on top of that I'm somehow supposed to come up with cash to actually buy these properties, too? What kind of normal person has that kind of cash just lying around? If I did, I wouldn't need to start a business in the first place!

At least Mark wasn't watching it with me. What would he think about spending tens of thousands of dollars that we don't even have on something so crazy?

Amy knew that last thought wasn't completely fair. Mark had been nothing but supportive of her wanting to start a business, even though their financial lives would be a lot easier if she was working right now. But as a lawyer, he had a finely tuned bullshit-o-meter, and that seminar would have kicked it right off the scale. Which is why it was just as well that Mark wasn't home last night.

He has been working late a lot lately. I wish he didn't have to. But everything is so expensive around here. He's been a prince carrying all this, and now I'm running out of time. Only two months left...

Amy sighed. She was heading into familiar territory now: feeling bad that her husband was working so hard, which leads to feeling bad about not pulling her weight, which leads to frustration and embarrassment about having been working at "starting a business" for close to a year now, with nothing to show for it. But she didn't have time to wallow.

Damn, I'm going to be late. I need to park, get in, get out, and get back on the road. I've been circling for ten minutes already – why is it so packed? Okay, think, Amy. Looking for a spot this close to the mall was a mistake – maybe I'll find one a little further out in the lot. I just need to–

Hey, what the–

Amy slammed on the brakes, just barely avoiding hitting the car that had pulled out in front of her. The driver behind her wasn't as quick. He drove right into her. Even at 15 miles per hour, there was enough force that Amy lurched forward. Her arm instinctively covered the steering wheel to brace for impact, sounding the horn.

As the car that pulled out in front of her sped away, Amy heard the door of the car behind her open.

"I'm so sorry!" The driver said as he approached her window. "Are you all right? Are you hurt?"

"I think I'm okay." Amy nodded, a bit shaken. "Are you all right?"

"I'm fine." He replied. "I'm so, so sorry."

Amy unbuckled her seatbelt and got out of the car to assess the damage. When she had bought the used Corolla earlier that year, it had been in perfect shape. Now, the rear bumper was a complete wreck. She looked over to the car that had inflicted the damage: a bright blue Tesla model 3 electric car. It barely had a scratch on it.

That figures.

"I'm so sorry about your car!" The man said. Amy could tell from his face that he meant it.

"I guess these things happen." Amy said, frustrated. "You have insurance, right?"

"Yes, of course." The man said. Amy thought she heard a hint of an accent, but couldn't place where it was from. "It's in the glove box, just a moment." He went over to his car, and returned a moment later with insurance papers. "I'll cover anything that the insurance won't, this was my fault. I should have stopped."

Wow, he really feels bad. Poor guy. I'm sure the insurance company will cover it.

"I appreciate that." Amy said, taking a better look at him. He looked to be in his early thirties, but the bags under his eyes made him look older. He was wearing cargo pants and a black t-shirt with a slogan across the front.

Life is short. Do stuff that matters. I like that.

Amy noticed a milk-colored stain on his left shoulder – the sort that a baby would make spitting up on you.

So that's it. He's a new father. That explains him being tired!

"Aren't those fancy electric cars supposed to have motion sensors to prevent stuff like this?" Amy asked.

"Yes, they do. The alarms went off right before I hit you." He replied sheepishly.

"I'm Amy, by the way." Amy extended her hand.

He shook it, and replied, "I'm Kevin. Here, do you want to take a photo of my insurance information?"

"Yeah, that works." Amy said, snapping a couple of photos of his insurance papers.

4

"I really am sorry, Amy." Kevin repeated. "I'm usually such a careful driver. I'm just so tired. Maybe I shouldn't even be driving."

"It's all right, it was an accident. But yeah, maybe better to Uber it until your baby is sleeping better." Amy said with a smile.

"How did you know?" Kevin asked.

"The spit-up stain on your shoulder is a dead giveaway."

"Oh, I hadn't even noticed. That's embarrassing." Kevin said, then shrugged. "But then, I guess you're past the point of impressing anyone when you've just rear-ended their car."

"It's okay – every parent has been there. How old is your baby?"

"Six weeks." Kevin replied.

"Ah, yeah, that makes sense. That's about the point where a lot of parents really start to crash. How are you handling it?" Amy asked.

"I mean, it's wonderful – I can't believe how much I love the little guy. He just started smiling, and it's the best thing in the world." Kevin started, then paused.

"Oh, that's early for the baby to be smiling. That's great. But that's not the whole story, is it?" Amy prodded.

"I mean, it's all good." Kevin started again, "But I'm just so tired, and my wife is a wreck. I don't know how people get through this."

"I know it's hard, but it really does get better. And listen, it doesn't have to be this hard." Amy paused for a moment, and then continued, "I can help, if you're willing?"

"How do you mean?" Kevin asked, a bit guarded.

"Oh, nothing weird. It's just that helping new parents get their babies to sleep is kind of my thing." Amy explained.

"For real? That's amazing. How do you do that?" Kevin asked.

"I have a whole process that I can teach you. It won't take long – maybe twenty minutes or so?"

"That's very kind of you to offer," Kevin replied, "especially considering what I just did to your car. Yes, absolutely, I'm ready to try anything."

"Okay, great. So look, I'm running late, but how about if we meet tomorrow morning? And you can bring your wife?" Amy suggested.

"That sounds great. Where should we meet you?" Kevin asked.

"Café Java, right over there?" Amy gestured to the café that could be seen past the rows of cars. "Around ten?"

"Absolutely. And thank you. Truly, I'm grateful."

"Well, I haven't helped you yet, but you're welcome. I'll see you tomorrow."

Chapter 2
AMY'S DAD

Half an hour later, Amy was on the road again. She run her errand as quickly as she could, but she was still running very late.

Okay, let's see. I'm supposed to get to the restaurant at half past noon, and it's a quarter to twelve now. Do I still have time to make it over to see dad?

Amy pondered for a moment. Given the detour, she'd only have about ten minutes to spend with her father. It almost seemed like it would be easier to drive straight to the restaurant, and catch up on a few emails in the parking lot.

No, what am I thinking? Nothing is more important than seeing dad. And I can be a bit late for lunch.

Amy set the address into the GPS out of habit, but the truth is that she could have found her way there in her sleep. She had grown up here, and even though a lot had changed, the whole area felt viscerally familiar.

Amy had left California to attend college in Ohio. She fully intended to graduate and come back home, but when she was a junior she met Mark, who had just started law school. It was a whirlwind romance and less than a year later they tied the knot. They agreed that Amy would take a year off to work while Mark finished law school, and then she'd go back to school and finish her degree. When she graduated, she was pregnant with Rick, and then a few years later Daisy came along. Mark was on the fast track at a bigtime environmental law firm. Life wasn't perfect, but it was pretty darn good. And while they had never actually decided not to move back to California, it just gradually faded out of their plans.

That is, until last year. She would never forget the phone call that had changed everything.

"Hello, Amy?" Amy knew from the caller ID that the voice on the other end of the line belonged to her father's assistant Rena, who had been an acquaintance of Amy's in high school.

"Rena! It's been a while. How are you doing? What's up?"

"Amy, it's your dad." Rena said, her voice a bit shaky. "He just collapsed. The paramedics are saying that it's a stroke..."

Amy couldn't remember the rest of the call, but that night she was in California, and three weeks later their house in Ohio was on the market. There was no question – for her, or for Mark – that it was time to move closer to family.

Amy backed into the driveway, the way her father had taught her years ago. She got out of the car, made her way up the walkway, and knocked on the door.

"Amy!" Rosa's voice greeted her as the door opened.

"Rosa!" Amy smiled and gave her a hug. Rosa had had moved next door to Amy when they were both six, and had been fast friends ever since. When Amy had moved to Ohio, Rosa had gone to nursing school, and trained as an in-home care provider. When she heard about Amy's dad's stroke, she asked to be assigned to him.

"How is he doing today?" Amy asked.

"I'm fine, Amy. Come give me a hug." Amy's father's voice called from the living room. David Tanley had been a sales executive at a small but successful shoe company. At 75, he was still going strong until the stroke forced him into what he still called "early retirement". Mentally, his recovery had been relatively quick, but physically the stroke had taken a heavy toll.

Amy went over, leaned down, and kissed him on the head.

"Hi dad. How are you doing today?"

"Well, I'm still in a wheelchair, so there's that." David said, with a twinkle in his eye. "But I haven't bumped into anything today. How about you?"

Amy realized that the living room window offered a perfect view of her car's badly damaged bumper. "Nothing gets by you, dad. Yeah, I got rear-ended in the Pacific Heights parking lot, right before I came over here. That's why I'm late. I can't stay long, but I wanted to see you."

"Are you okay?" David asked.

"Yeah, I'm fine. Just a bit frazzled. Insurance will take care of it, and the guy was actually really nice." Amy explained.

"Do you need some money to get it fixed in the meantime, until the insurance company pays up?" David asked.

"No, dad, Mark and I are fine. But thank you." Amy

didn't like the idea of taking money from her father, and anyway she knew that he was as stretched as she was; he had worked a good job and been diligent about saving, but the healthcare costs had changed everything.

"Are you sure, honey?" David asked again.

"I'm sure, dad." Amy said with a smile. "Really, we're fine."

"All right. Then tell me about your business. What are you working on right now?" Amy knew that her father was genuinely interested, and when she had started down this path she would tell him about every idea. That was before she realized that being an entrepreneur sometimes means getting excited about a different idea each week until you find the 'right' one... and then having the 'right' one turn out to be the wrong one, and start the cycle all over again. To a lot of people, it just looked flighty. So Amy had learned to be a little more cautious about sharing. Not that he was unsupportive – but like any daughter, she wanted her father to see her as competent and capable.

Competent and capable... yeah, right. With the results I've had this year, I don't look like either of those things. I'll tell him when something pans out.

But David knew his daughter. "Amy, what's the matter? Did something happen with your work?"

"No, nothing happened, and I've got something in the works. I'll tell you about it in a few weeks if it works out. It's more that..." Amy's voice trailed off.

"What is it, honey?" David prodded gently.

"I guess I just wonder sometimes... am I kidding myself?" Amy began, "I mean, with the whole idea of starting a business, setting my own hours, being able to come here every day. Mark is working so hard, and being crammed into that tiny apartment has been rough on the kids... sometimes I just wonder if I should give up on the pipe dream and find a job. Then I have this feeling, that it wouldn't be enough, like I'm meant for more than that. I know, I sound so obnoxious right now."

"Obnoxious? Honey, what are you talking about?" David asked.

"Well, there are a lot of people struggling right now to keep a roof over their heads. To find one decent job. And Mark has a good job, but everything around here is just so expensive. Maybe I'm not 'meant for more' – maybe I should just find something, bring in a decent paycheck to take the pressure off of Mark and let us move into a place that isn't so cramped. Maybe I should just be satisfied with that?"

"Amy, come on. You aren't trying to start a business to pay for a fancy car collection. You're doing it to help people. Like your husband, and your kids. And me. Not every daughter would move across the country to be closer to her sick dad. And take it from your sick dad. I've known you for your whole life, and you are absolutely meant for more. But that doesn't mean it'll be easy to get there. It's supposed to be hard – if it was easy, anyone could do it. And starting a business, creating that freedom... it isn't easy. Anyone can't do it. But I know you Amy, and you, you can do it."

Amy paused for a long moment. "Thank you, dad. I know this much, I don't think I could do it if I didn't have you as my cheerleader."

"Well, I think you could do that too, but we won't have to find that out." David said with another grin. "Hey, you said that you had to go, didn't you?"

Amy glanced at the old grandfather clock that she had been there since she was a child. "Oh, shoot. Yes, I do." Amy hugged her father. "I'll be back tomorrow. Rosa, could you walk me out?"

"Sure." Rosa said.

When they got to the car, Rosa winced. "Wow, that guy really did a number on your car!"

"Yeah, I know." Amy said, and then looked intently at her friend. "Rosa, tell me really, how is he doing?"

"Amy, you know your dad," Rosa began, "he wouldn't complain if his legs were on fire. But I can tell he's frustrated about the things that he can't do anymore."

"I know. I wish there was more that I could be doing." Amy said.

"Amy, you're here every day. That's a lot, and it really makes a difference."

Chapter 3
MASTERMIND

Twenty minutes later, Amy walked into the Jamaican Kitchen restaurant. Lunch wasn't their busy time, so the restaurant was quiet, but Amy could smell the richly spiced aroma of Caribbean food.

Mmmm, that smells delicious.

Amy quickly scanned the dining room to find her friends, who were already seated. She made her way over, waving as she approached.

"Hi guys, so sorry I'm late. It's been a weird morning – I got rear-ended in the Pacific Heights parking lot!" Amy explained as she sat down. "I'm fine, and the guy was really apologetic." She continued, waving away the concerned looks on her friends' faces. "It's just been a weird morning, that's all."

"No worries." Tamara replied. "Are you sure you're okay?" Even though she'd lived in the United States since she was a teenager, she still had a Jamaican accent. Amy had met her by chance at a bookstore the week after moving back to California, and they had become fast friends. And when Tamara learned that Amy was thinking about starting a business, she invited her into her lunch mastermind group.

"Yeah, really, I'm fine. Just a bit frazzled." Amy said, taking a deep breath. "Have you guys started already?"

"Nah, we were just catching up, and I was showing off my henna." Devi said, raising two elaborately decorated hands.

"Oh, I forgot that was this week. Is your sister excited?" Amy asked. Even though the lunches were focused on the businesses that each of the four people were trying to start, real friendships had developed.

"Yup, super excited. And things are so busy – you know how Indian weddings are!" Devi replied.

"We know from what you've told us! Wow, that's just gorgeous. Did you do it yourself?" Tom asked, his voice tinged with just a hint of a Southern accent. He was the only man at the table, and quite a bit older than the others. But he was a gentle soul, and he fit right in.

"No, I don't think I could manage that on my own hands. My cousin and I did the art for everyone, so she did mine and I did hers."

Just then the server came by, and orders were placed for jerk chicken, pepper pot soup, and callaloo. Then they all looked at each other expectantly.

"All right ladies, should we get to it?" Tom asked, "How about if we do the Reader's Digest version of our updates, so we can jump right in?" The others nodded, so Tom continued,

"Tamara, since you're here with us this time, why don't you go first?"

"Well, I couldn't miss it on my turn to pick the restaurant, could I?" Tamara said with a guilty smile. Even though she had been the one who first put the group together, she was also the one who missed the most meetings. "But I take your point, I've been traveling a lot. But I mean, that's why I'm doing this." Tamara was an independent management consultant, which basically meant that companies paid her huge amounts of money to fly in and tell them how to solve their problems. Which was great, except that she was on the road more often than she was home. That's why she was trying to figure out a way to make money that didn't take her away from home quite as much. "So as you know, I'm trying to get speaking gigs." Tamara figured that if she were speaking instead of consulting, the trips would at least be a lot shorter. "Last time I committed to reach out to ten of my past clients and ask if they were looking for speakers for their corporate events. Which I did."

This was the format of their meetings; every month the four of them would meet, and share how the last couple of weeks had gone. Then they'd share what they're thinking about doing next, and discuss options and ideas. Finally, each would make commitments for what they'd do in the coming weeks, that they'd have to report on at the next meeting.

"And how did it go? What did they say?" Amy asked.

"Well, I guess it worked out well. Two of them said I could do a lunch and learn for their teams. They're not paying me, but you have to start somewhere, right?"

"That's a great start, Tamara. Way to go." Devi said, squeezing her arm.

"Thanks. And I got another consulting gig – one of the clients I reached out to asked if I could come in to do some stuff for them."

"That's great." Tom said. "Why so glum?"

"Well, the money's good, so for sure I'll do it. But I was hoping to really focus on developing my talk for the next few weeks. Now it looks like I'll be flying back and forth to Atlanta. And, I think I'm going to miss our next meeting." Tamara felt defeated, but also uncomfortable about feeling defeated. Having too many people wanting to pay her giant sums of money didn't feel like something she should complain about.

"Tamara, it's great. It's progress, you're building momentum." Amy said.

"Thanks, hon." Tamara said with a wan smile. "Tom, you want to go next?"

"Sure. I was supposed to look for suppliers for those basketballs I'm going to sell."

"Hang on, I think I missed something. What basketballs?" Amy asked.

"Oh, right, you weren't here last time. So what I'm trying to do is this thing called drop-shipping. Basically, I'd get a product manufactured and sent straight to Amazon warehouses, so people could buy them online. I looked at a bunch of products, and it looks like basketballs cost twenty or thirty bucks on Amazon, and sometimes more than that. But they only cost a few bucks to make, and there's no risk of them breaking in transit. So if I can get them made with interesting designs on them, maybe I can stand out." Tom had been a massage therapist for the past forty years, and he was very good at it – as Amy learned when she threw out her back two months ago, and called him for help. But he was starting to feel his age, and didn't think he'd be able to continue doing manual work for too much longer – at least not full-time. Would this drop-shipping idea be his ticket to freedom? "So anyway, I was supposed to look for suppliers for those basketballs. You know, factories in China."

"That's really cool. So how did you do?" Amy asked.

"Not as well as I'd like." Tom said, a little bit sheepish and a little bit frustrated. "I thought there'd be something like a Yellow Pages for these things, but it isn't that simple. You've got to cruise sites like Alibaba to look for suppliers, and then you start a conversation and make a sample order. I don't want to spend a ton of money just to find a good supplier, though, so I'm taking it slow."

"That makes sense." Devi said. "It sounds like a long process, though. I mean, you find a supplier, they ship the sample to you... that all takes time. So maybe it makes sense to try two or three of them at the same time, to hedge your bets?"

"Yeah, that's what I was thinking, but I wanted to check with you ladies to make sure I'm not rushing things. Does that sound right to y'all?" The women around the table all nodded. "All right then, I think I got what I came for! Devi, you want to go next?"

"Sure, but I don't have that much to report. I'm working through my copywriting program and getting involved in copywriter communities, but no gigs yet." Devi worked in cyber-security, but hated the long hours. She was trying to start a side hustle where she'd get paid to write marketing emails and web pages for clients. Supposedly, good copywriters were very well paid, and had great flexibility with their schedules. "Amy, what about you?"

All eyes turned to Amy, and she felt her heart start beating faster. Even though these were all friends, she still felt nervous talking in front of people. "Well, first of all, I promised I'd tell you guys about that webinar yesterday on buying and selling distressed real estate – that was a bust."

"That's too bad. But we figured that it was a long shot, right?" Tom asked.

"Yeah, for sure, and it was my turn. You did the cryptocurrency one last month, so fair is fair."

"There's enough stuff out there that we all get a turn." Devi said with a grin. "But that isn't your main thing. What about the affiliate marketing plan you've been working on?"

"Yeah, I actually made some good progress on that." Amy replied. "So remember, affiliate marketing is basically doing the marketing for somebody else's products, and earning a commission on the sale. Last time I said that I was looking at different offers that I could promote, and I found one: this company called VitaMagic Smoothies. Basically they send you this green powder that you put in your daily smoothie to keep you healthy."

"So you're going to do marketing for this smoothie product?" Tamara asked.

"Yup. It looks really solid. I'll promote their monthly

subscription, and I get $100 for every person who signs up." Amy explained.

"Nice. And you're going to do the marketing on Facebook?" Tom asked.

"That's right. I'm a little worried that it won't work, but I'm setting the budget to $15/day, so I figure it's not that much of a risk. I'll let it run for a couple of weeks. If it works, that's great, and if not, that's just two hundred bucks, so it wouldn't be the end of the world."

"How many ads are you going to run?" Devi asked.

"I've written a dozen different ones. The ad system is supposed to rotate them, and spend the budget on whichever ad is working best." Amy explained.

"It sounds like you've really thought this through, Amy. That's exciting – I hope it works out!" Tamara said, giving Amy's arm a squeeze.

"Me too. Honestly, I'm feeling nervous."

"About the ads? It's like you said, you aren't risking that much." Tamara reassured her.

"No, it's not the ads, it's just how fast the time is going. I told you guys that when Mark and I moved back to California, we made a deal that I'd spend a year trying to figure out something with starting a business, and if that doesn't work I'd get a job. Which I guess wouldn't be the end of the world, but I really love that I can visit my dad every day, and I won't be able to do that anymore. I've only got two months left, so I feel like I'm running out of time."

"I hear you, hon." Tamara said. "We all want this to go faster than it is, but you're doing the best you can. We all are.

It's a really great thing you're doing, spending so much time with your dad. And look, the ads could work. Next month we could all be celebrating your success!"

"Thanks Tamara. I really hope so." Amy answered, as the server arrived with their lunch orders. The dishes were placed on the table, and they chatted as they began to eat.

Amy tried to enjoy the food and conversation, but she couldn't take her mind off of the looming deadline.

I really hope this works out!

Chapter 4

AMY'S 'LITTLE' FORMULA

The next morning, Amy was sitting in a booth at Café Java. She had arrived early for the meeting with Kevin, and ordered a cup of tea. Kevin arrived a few minutes past the hour, awkwardly holding a baby carrier in one hand.

Amy waved him over. "Good morning!"

"Good morning." Kevin replied as he gently lowered the carrier into the booth. "This is Liam."

"He's adorable." Amy said, smiling. "Isn't it amazing how peaceful they look when they're asleep?"

"Yup. It's a hell of a contrast." Kevin said. If anything, the bags under his eyes seemed to have gotten larger.

"Where's your wife?" Amy asked.

"Alyssa was so tired this morning, I figured I'd let her sleep." Kevin explained.

"That's thoughtful."

"Oh, it's the least I can do. This has been hard for me, but it's been a lot harder for her." Kevin replied. Just then a server walked by the table, and Kevin raised his arm to flag her. "Excuse me, I'll have a triple espresso, please."

"That bad?" Amy asked.

"Yeah, it's been rough. Especially that I've been working, more or less, in parallel with all this going on."

"Oh? What do you do?" Amy asked.

"I teach online marketing." Kevin explained. "I work from home, so there's a fair amount of flexibility. But it's crazy how long things seem to take when you're this tired, and taking care of a baby at the same time. It's like things that I used to be able to do in twenty minutes take four hours now. I'm not even exaggerating."

"The first couple of months are really tough." Amy commiserated. "With any kid, but especially with the first. It's not just that they aren't sleeping, it's also such a big adjustment that you can't really prepare for."

"I know what you mean. I must have read a dozen books about being a new parent, so I figured I had this handled. Boy, was I wrong."

"It gets easier, though," Amy explained, "especially once they start sleeping a bit better. Which I can help you with."

"Well, I'm excited to hear about this. You help people get their babies to sleep?" Kevin asked.

"Yeah, it's something I've been doing since my kids were little. My first was a terrible sleeper, I mean world record setting terrible. So I had to figure this out. And at first I thought he was just a special case, but once I had something that works, I found myself explaining it to other moms, and they said it worked for them, too." Amy was getting into full teacher mode now. "It's actually pretty simple. I call it my 'Little' formula for getting babies to sleep, because I use the acronym L-T-L. The first L is for Light, as in you don't want any light at all. It's got to be completely dark in the baby's room. Is that how you've got it setup right now?"

"No, there's a big window with sheer curtains. And we have a lamp that projects stars onto the ceiling for night time." Kevin replied. "I thought babies are afraid of the dark?"

"No, that comes later. When they're four or five, they'll want a night light. But right now, you want it to be completely dark. So get rid of that lamp, and order blackout curtains from Amazon." Amy instructed.

Kevin pulled out his phone, tapped on it a few times, and held it up to show Amy. "Like these?"

Amy looked at the Amazon product listing, and nodded. "Exactly."

"Done – ordered. I should be able to put them up tomorrow." Kevin said, happy to be taking some sort of action. "Okay, what's next?"

"So the first L is light, and then comes the T, which is for Tight. The baby needs to be swaddled super tight." Amy glanced over at the sleeping baby. "You see that? He's too loose in there. It needs to be really tight, like a burrito."

"I know, I read about that." Kevin explained. "I wrap him up tight, but in two minutes the little guy has wriggled out of it. It's like he's a baby Houdini."

"Yeah, they're good at that, especially when they're agitated. But look, you're using the wrong wraps. You want to use a muslin swaddling blanket – you stretch it a bit while you do the wrapping, so it holds tight."

Kevin picked up his phone again. "Do I spell that with an O or a U?"

"Muslin is with an U." Amy replied.

"Got it. Like this?" Kevin held up his phone for Amy.

"Yup, that's perfect."

"Great. I'll have those tomorrow, too." Kevin said, putting his phone down again.

"Okay. So the first L is for Light, and the T is for Tight. The second L is for Loud." Amy explained.

"Oh, his room is totally quiet. You could hear a pin drop." Kevin said, frustrated.

Amy interrupted him. "No, it's the opposite of that. You actually want it to be loud."

"What do you mean? How could anyone sleep if it's loud?" Kevin asked.

"Here's the thing." Amy explained. "This whole process is about simulating the womb, which is where the baby had been sleeping for the nine months before it was born. In there it was dark, cramped, and loud. There was noise from the outside, and also all the sounds from inside your wife's body – her digestion, her pulse. It was like sleeping at a dance party in there."

"Oh, wow, I never thought of that." Kevin said, surprised. "So I should put on some music for him?"

"No, not exactly. You want to find a white noise machine. Something that's loud but consistent, so it doesn't startle him. Here, give me your phone." Amy said, reaching out her hand.

Kevin handed her the phone, and she opened up a listing for the white noise machine that she recommended to her friends.

"This is great – thank you." Kevin said, and ordered the device.

"It's really that simple. Light, Tight, and Loud. My 'Little' Formula." Amy said, grinning. "Try it tonight. Or I guess tomorrow, once you get all this gear. You'll see the difference."

"And you learned all this just from figuring out how to put your baby to sleep?" Kevin asked.

"Well, that's how it started. But I find this stuff really fascinating, so I ended up reading a lot more about it than I probably needed, and I took some classes about child development. Nothing too serious, but it's definitely helped me help a whole bunch of moms over the years."

"That's really cool. Thank you for sharing this. I know I haven't tried it yet, but I feel like there's a light at the end of the tunnel now." Kevin said, grateful. He reached into his pocket, and pulled out his wallet. "How much do I owe you?"

"Oh, you don't have to pay me! This was just friendly advice." Amy said, surprised.

"Are you sure?" Kevin asked.

"Yes, of course. It's not like I'm a real expert or anything."

Kevin put away his wallet. "In that case, I'll just say thank you. Really, thank you."

"You're very welcome." Amy smiled.

"Listen," Kevin asked, "I've got to do something to thank you. Would you and your husband come over for dinner next week?"

"That's sweet of you to offer," Amy protested, "but we wouldn't want to impose."

"Come on, it's the least I can do." Kevin insisted.

"Are you sure? I know how hectic it is with a new baby around." Amy asked.

"Well, don't get me wrong – it won't be anything fancy. It might even be takeout. But we'd love to have you over. Really."

"Then we'd be very happy to." Amy agreed. "Text me the details, and Mark and I will look forward to meeting Alyssa."

Chapter 5

DINNER

Less than a week later, Amy and Mark were sitting in Kevin's living room, meeting his wife Alyssa. Amy noticed that Kevin didn't look quite as tired as he did when they had met at Café Java.

"You look more rested than the last time I saw you." Amy commented. "How has Liam been sleeping?"

Kevin was about to answer, but Alyssa beat him to it. "A lot better. Thank you so, so much."

"Oh, I'm so glad to hear that!" Amy said with big smile.

"It's a world of difference for us." Kevin explained. "He's sleeping almost four hours at a stretch, instead of waking up every couple of hours. So we're doing it in shifts, and we can both get a halfway decent night's sleep. I feel like I've been coming out of a fog these last few days."

"I know, it's crazy how fast our world turns upside down when we can't sleep. I read somewhere that missing a couple hours of sleep is the same as driving drunk. So just imagine the effect of the weeks or months of chronic sleep deprivation that new parents go through!" Amy said.

"Yeah, no wonder I hit you." Kevin said, then realized it was probably too soon to be making jokes. "Which again, I'm really sorry about."

"It's okay." Mark interjected. "Maybe it was meant to be – otherwise we wouldn't have met, right?"

"That's really generous of you to say, Mark. And yeah, I really hate to think how Alyssa and I would be feeling right now without Amy's help." Kevin said with a shudder. "It would have been bad."

"It's amazing that just a few tweaks to Liam's room could make such a difference!" Alyssa added.

"Yup, plus the movement piece, right?" Mark said.

"The movement piece?" Kevin asked.

"I actually didn't teach Kevin that part yet." Amy said. "It's not exactly about the sleep environment, so I don't see it as part of the formula. It's extra."

"And there's no M in little, right?" Mark teased his wife.

"Yeah, maybe that's a part of it." Amy said with a smile. "But yeah, there's an add-on to my formula, it's M for movement. If Liam is really struggling to sleep, or just very upset, you should lay him across your knee and jiggle very gently, just enough for his head to bob a little bit. The movement will help put him to sleep."

"Cool – got it." Kevin said. "He just went down, but if he wakes up when you're still here, maybe we can try it and you can tell us if we're doing it right?"

"Sure." Amy replied. "And if not, you can always call me later. I'll make sure you're getting it right."

Just then a 'ding' sounded from the kitchen.

"Dinner is ready." Alyssa said. "Shall we sit down?"

The four made their way to the dining room table, and Alyssa brought out a simple but delicious smelling pasta dish, and a salad.

"It's nothing fancy." Alyssa said apologetically.

"It smells great." Mark said. "And you've got a newborn. If this was our place right after Rick or Daisy was born, we wouldn't even have clean dishes!"

Alyssa nodded with appreciation as they all began to eat.

"So what do you both do?" Mark asked.

"I work in HR at a tech startup." Alyssa said. "But I'm off for mat leave, of course. The company has good benefits."

"Cool. What about you, Kevin?" Mark asked.

"I teach online business." Kevin replied.

"Like, at the university?" Mark prodded.

"No, I work for myself. I have clients that I advise, and online courses that I run a few times each year." Kevin explained.

"Oh, that's interesting. Amy, have you spoken with Kevin about what you're trying to do?" Mark asked his wife.

"What are you working on, Amy?" Kevin asked.

"Well, when Mark and I moved here from Ohio, I thought I could try to figure out some way of making money online instead of finding a job, so I'd have more time to be with my family." Amy explained.

"That's great. What sort of business are you building?" Kevin asked.

"Well, to be honest, I'm still figuring out what the right thing is for me. I've experimented with a few things, but all the things I've tried either didn't feel right, or didn't end up working." Amy shared, demoralized.

"For what it's worth, that's pretty normal. It's a big world of opportunities, and it takes some exploration to find the one that feels right to you. And it doesn't help that there's a lot of snake oil in this industry..." Kevin said.

"That's been my impression." Mark agreed.

"It's not all snake oil, though." Amy said defensively. "Some of these ideas are good, they're just hard to make work. And online platforms are changing quickly, so by the time I think I've wrapped my head around something, things have changed."

"I know that honey. I wasn't criticizing, just agreeing that it seems hard to separate the wheat from the chaff." Mark said.

"That's true. And I know I don't need to be defensive. Mark has been super supportive." Amy said, gesturing with appreciation to her husband. "Truth be told, I just feel frustrated about how slowly things seem to be moving. But I've got something I'm working on that I feel good about."

"That's great." Kevin said. "Listen, if you have any questions or need any help with this stuff, it's what I help people do every day. I'm more than happy to lend an ear – it's the least I could do, after your help with Liam. Not to mention that I rear-ended you!"

"I appreciate that, and I might take you up on it. But I don't want to impose. This is what you do for a living." Amy said.

"Really, I'd be happy to. But look, here's what a lot of this comes down to: you need to find something to sell that people really, really want to buy." Kevin began to explain. "Like the baby sleep stuff. We met under less-than-ideal circumstances, and I jumped on your offer to get help, because I was desperate. It was very kind of you to help as a favor, but I would have been very happy to pay for that help."

"Right, but I'm not a real expert. I can't charge people money for this stuff." Amy said, resistant to the idea.

"Why not? I mean, why do you say that you aren't an expert?" Kevin asked.

"Well, I'm not a doctor, I don't have a PhD... I'm not an expert." Amy said.

"I don't see it that way." Kevin said. "Not about being a doctor or having a PhD, I believe you don't have those. But you do have expertise that I don't, and that was valuable to me. Expertise that comes from study, practice, and real-life experience. Expertise that you've validated through study and trial and error over the course of a decade and a half. Isn't that right?"

"I guess it is." Amy replied.

"Well, that makes you an expert. And of course, you need to be up-front and honest about the limitations of your expertise, and not claim to have knowledge that you don't have. But speaking as a person who has legitimately benefited from the stuff that took you decades to figure out, that's real expertise, and it's valuable." Kevin could see that Amy was feeling uncomfortable, so he decided not to push further. "Anyway, I think there's something there. If you ever want to talk about it, I'm more than happy to help."

The conversation continued, and both couples enjoyed the evening. For Amy and Mark, it was a fun connection with an interesting couple. It was also that for Kevin and Alyssa, and also their first opportunity in six weeks to have a relaxed conversation with other adults.

After they had all finished their meals and enjoyed a warm beverage (tea for Amy, and coffee for the others), Alyssa brought out a few Tupperware containers, and began to put away the leftover food. Which sparked a thought for Mark.

"Hey Alyssa, on an unrelated subject," Mark began, "can I ask your opinion about something?"

"Sure, what is it?" Alyssa asked.

"These Tupperwares," Mark said, gesturing at the plastic food containers, "after you use them, do you wash them by hand, or put them in the dishwasher?"

Amy cast an exasperated glance at Mark, but Alyssa didn't notice.

"I guess it depends on who ends up doing it. Kevin likes to wash everything by hand." Alyssa said, gesturing at her husband.

"It's true." Kevin said with a shrug. "There's something meditative about washing dishes, and I like the feeling that no matter how big the mess in the sink, I can completely fix it in half an hour, or an hour tops."

"It gives him a sense of control." Alyssa explained.

"Though, to be fair, since the baby we've been using the dishwasher a lot more." Kevin added.

"Sure, that makes sense. But okay, here's my real question: when you put the Tupperwares in the dishwasher, do you put them on the top drawer, or the bottom drawer?" Mark asked.

Alyssa thought for a moment, and then replied. "I usually put them on the top. I think I heard somewhere that you're supposed to put them on the top, because of something about the temperature or the water flow interacting with the plastic. Is that right?"

"Yes, exactly." Mark said with a wide grin.

"Okay, we have to explain this." Amy said with a wry smile. "Mark has this fixation on only putting plastics on the top shelf. I do that when I can, but mostly I just put them wherever there's room. And it drives him up the wall for some reason."

"It's true, I'm too sensitive about it. It's just one of those things." Mark said with a shrug. "Maybe it's the lawyer in me wanting everything to be precise."

"So anyway, it's become a sort of running joke between us, and we ask new people we meet. So I guess you're on Team Mark." Amy said explained.

"Which team is winning?" Kevin asked.

"So far it's pretty close to even." Mark replied.

They chatted for a few more minutes, and then said their farewells.

It had been a pleasant evening, with the conversation veering in the direction of childhood stories, what brought both families to California, favorite haunts in the city, and of course the experience of new parenthood.

But hours later, when Amy was lying awake in bed thinking about the evening, it was Kevin's business suggestion that occupied her thoughts.

Chapter 6
THE BABY MANUAL

The next morning, once Mark and the kids were off to work and school, Amy prepared a cup of tea as she pondered Kevin's suggestion from the previous night.

Maybe I could create a product to teach about all the baby stuff. I mean, there is so much that new parents don't know, even in the first year. In the first six months!

She sighed.

But who am I to teach that stuff? There are so many books out there for new parents. By doctors, researchers... real experts.

But Kevin's words from the night before still rang in her mind: "You have expertise that I don't, and that was valuable to me. Expertise that comes from study, practice, and real-life experience. Expertise that you've validated over the course of decades."

Maybe it's worth a shot. At least I'd be dealing with an area that I know something about, instead of trying to puzzle out social media platforms that I don't understand. And it does feel really good when I help a new parent get their baby to sleep – like I'm really making a difference for them. How great would it be if I could actually make money doing that?

Amy took a deep breath, and committed.

Okay, let's do this. But what is "this"? I can't just start charging people for giving them advice, that would feel awkward. Advice doesn't cost me anything to give, so it would be weird to try to charge people for it. Because whatever Kevin says, I'm not a doctor! But I could write down the procedure, and sell that.

Amy shook her head.

No, that doesn't work. I could explain the Little Formula in just a few pages, and you can't sell a few pages of text – that's an article! So I need more than just the sleep thing. But it's not just sleep that's hard for new parents, it's everything. If you've never had a baby before, your whole life changes, and you don't know how to take care of this little person.

Amy smiled as she thought back to the first few months after Rick was born, almost 17 years ago.

I didn't know a thing – and I felt so overwhelmed! If I could teach new parents about all the things that come up in those first few months, that might be valuable.

Amy nodded to herself, pleased with the idea.

Okay, that's it. A guidebook for the first few months of being a parent. That just might work!

She opened a fresh Word document, and typed a title in bold face: "The Baby Manual."

Chapter 7
RUNNING

Thoop. Thoop. Thoop. Thoop.

Running was Amy's escape. With every step, she felt a hair further removed from her troubles, and a hair closer to herself. So when something went terribly wrong, her first instinct was to grab her sneakers and head out the door.

Thoop. Thoop. Thoop. Thoop.

And boy, did things ever seem terribly wrong. It had been a month since she began work on her manual for new parents. Despite her enthusiasm, her progress had been slow as she wrestled to define the scope of the project. Would this manual focus on the first month, or the first six months? Was it primarily about the baby, or about the parents? Speaking of parents, was this manual meant for mom, or for dad? Each of these choices had implications about what would or wouldn't be included, and what examples and anecdotes would be relevant and compelling. So the days turned into weeks as Amy revised and adjusted an outline, without so much as a page of actual text to show for it.

Thoop. Thoop. Thoop. Thoop.

As if the stalled manual and fast approaching deadline to make this whole entrepreneurship adventure work weren't enough, there was another problem. This was what had actually set Amy out on this run. Amy grunted with frustration, and accelerated her pace.

Thoop. Thoop. Thoop. Thoop. Thoop. Thoop.

This morning, the family credit card bill had arrived. She opened the envelope, and was stunned by a bill for thousands of dollars more than she had been expecting. Amy's first thought was that her son Rick had used the card to buy something extravagant, but her fury turned to horror as she realized that she was the culprit.

Thoop. Thoop. Thoop. Thoop. Thoop. Thoop.

The outsized charge was for the Facebook ads that she had run for the VitaMagic Smoothies company. She had made two small but significant mistakes. Her first error was in setting her daily budget. She thought it was set to $15 per day for the whole project, but she had actually set a $15 daily budget for each of the dozen ads that she had written. And second, in her excitement (and then frustration) with the baby manual project, she had forgotten about the ads altogether. That is, until this morning, when she got the bill for thousands of dollars. And, adding insult to injury, the whole campaign had only resulted in three sales of the VitaMagic Smoothies product.

Thoop. Thoop. Thoop. Thoop. Thoop. Thoop.

I can't believe I did this! How could I be so stupid? Why didn't I check it after I set it up? Why didn't I check it a week later? Why wasn't I checking it every week?

Thousands of dollars would be a big-but-not-crippling hit to the Morgan family finances. It would hurt, but it wouldn't put them out of a home. But even worse than the financial impact was the prospect of facing Mark and telling him what she had done.

He's been supporting me for almost a year, and what am I bringing to the table? Nothing. Absolutely nothing.

After a year of failed efforts, Amy felt defeated. With this cataclysmic screw-up, she felt humiliated. And she had no one to blame but herself.

Thoop. Thoop. Thoop. Thoop. Thoop. Thoop.

Amy played the critical moments over and over again, and her mind spun out every imaginable scenario that could unfold once she fessed up to her mistake. All humiliating. All signifying defeat. All a bold statement to everyone she loved that she didn't measure up, and didn't have what it takes to make this dream a reality.

In that moment it was more than Amy was ready to face, so she just kept on running.

Chapter 8
BACK TO THE MASTERMIND

E ventually, Amy made her way back to the apartment. She took a shower and got dressed. She glanced at her watch, and realized that she was running late.

As luck would have it, her mastermind was meeting today. She was so embarrassed that she considered skipping the meeting, but then she reminded herself that situations like this are precisely what the mastermind was for. Tamara, Devi and Tom had all become friends and confidantes, and that's exactly what she needed right now.

Amy took a deep breath, steeled herself, and headed out the door.

This time they were meeting at Bombay Palace. Walking in, Amy was greeted by the scents of curry and cardamom. Ordinarily she would have taken a moment to savor it, but she was too focused on her situation to enjoy aroma of one of her favorite cuisines. She walked over to her friends, who were already seated.

"Hey Amy, you made it!" Devi greeted her with a smile.

"We were just getting ready to order. You know Indian food – do you know what you want?" Tamara asked.

"Um, yeah, sure." Amy said as she sat down.

Tom was the first to notice Amy's troubled expression. "Amy, what's wrong?" He asked. All eyes turned to her.

She took a deep breath, and began. "Guys, I really messed up."

For the next half hour, with short pauses only when the server came to take their lunch order, Amy told her friends about being stalled on the manual, and about the screw up with the ads. Her intention had been to stick to the specifics of the problem, but once she began sharing the floodgates were opened, and all her fears and insecurities poured out. By the time the food arrived, everything was on the proverbial table.

Amy dabbed her eyes with the tissue that Tamara had helpfully offered, and took a deep breath. "Thanks for listening, you guys. I feel a bit better just saying it all out loud. But now I need a plan. What am I going to do?"

"Well, let's talk through this all." Tamara jumped in, swinging naturally into business consultant mode. "You've got four problems: the ads, the manual, telling Mark, and figuring out what to do next. Right?"

Amy appreciated her friend's talent for getting to the heart of the matter. "Yeah, I guess that's right." She replied.

"Okay, let's start with the easy stuff." Tamara suggested, immediately regretting her choice of words.

"Easy? None of this is easy!" Amy said, frustrated.

"No, hon, it isn't easy." Devi said, reassuringly. "Maybe Tamara meant..."

"Simple." Tamara jumped in. "Not easy, but simple. As in, it's pretty straight-forward what to do."

"How do you mean?" Amy asked.

"Well, in terms of the money you lost on the ads, there's nothing you can do, right? There's no way to get that money back or anything, and that's okay – I mean it sucks, but you're not going to lose your apartment over it. Right?" Tamara paused to check with Amy.

"I guess you're right. There's nothing to be done other than to turn off the ads, which I already did." Amy said, nodding.

"Okay. And with Mark it's simple too, isn't it? I mean, it's going to be awful telling him, but is there any other choice?" Tamara asked.

"No, you're right. I can't not tell him. That's not how our marriage works." Amy nodded. Her friend was right; so far, the solutions weren't exactly easy, but they were simple – at least in the sense that there was an obvious next step, and not a lot of options.

"Amy, maybe we should talk a bit more about telling Mark." Devi suggested. "Not about whether you should, because of course you should. But about how to tell him, and how you feel about it?"

"That's the part I'm dreading." Amy admitted. "He's been so good through all of this – really carrying a lot. I know I really let him down."

"Amy," Tom gently interjected, "from everything you've

told us about Mark, he loves you. This was an honest mistake. A big mistake, but an honest one. I don't know him, but from your stories, it sounds like he'll understand."

"What about your deadline?" Devi asked. "You've got another month left, right?"

"Yeah, about a month. Which I guess is the other two problems, the manual and the figuring out what to do next." Amy sighed. "But what can I possibly do in a month, if I haven't been able to figure anything out in almost a year? Is this the end of the line? Do I need to just give this up?"

"A month isn't very long, that's true." Tom said. "But I do think you can get this done. And there's a real need for something like this. It was decades ago, and I still remember what it's like to be a new parent. You feel clueless, and terrified. And now it's even worse, because everyone's comparing themselves to what they see on social media, and thinks that all their friends have got it all figured out."

"I agree with Tom." Tamara added. "I would have loved a guidebook to helping with my kids when they were younger. For that matter, now that they're teenagers, I'd still love to have a guidebook!"

"Can I make a suggestion?" Devi asked. When Amy nodded, she continued. "All these things that you're having trouble deciding, like whether your manual is about the first month or the first six months, whether it's about the baby or about the parents, whether it's for mom or dad... what if you just make a list of all those decisions you have to make, and go through the list one by one and choose one. It doesn't have to be the right one, it just has to not be the wrong one. You know what I mean?"

"No, I don't think so. If it isn't the wrong one, doesn't it make it the right one?" Amy asked.

"Here's what I mean. Let's pretend you want a latte – you can get that with regular milk, or with almond, soy, or coconut milk. Right?" Amy nodded, and Devi continued. "There's probably a milk that is best for you – whichever you like the flavor and texture the absolute best. So one of them is the right answer for you, and if you haven't tried them all you won't know which without doing taste tests. Right?"

"It's worse than that, because the different brands all taste different. So you might like the almost milk better at one place, and the coconut milk better at another." Tom added.

Amy nodded. "Yeah, I get it. So there's a right one, and I don't know which it is. That's the problem I have with all these choices. I don't know what the right answer is, and I don't even know what I'd need to know to find out the right answer."

"Yup, exactly." Devi continued. "But let's stick with the latte example for another moment. What if we say that you're lactose intolerant. In that case we still don't know what the right choice is, but we do know what the wrong one is. Does that make sense?"

"Yeah, I get it." Amy said. "The regular cow milk is the wrong choice, because it will make me feel bad. So I don't know which of the other milks is the right one, but I do know that I can't choose the cow milk, because that's the wrong one. If I'm lactose intolerant."

"Exactly. So for all these choices that you have to make, you don't need to worry about finding the exact right answer, you just need to avoid obvious wrong ones. And if there are different options that aren't wrong, you just choose one and move on." Devi explained.

"Okay. So how do I know if something is the wrong option?" Amy asked.

"Well, if you know that you can't do it, it would be the wrong choice for you." Devi began. "Like, if you were choosing whether to make this about babies in general, or babies who have a specific medical condition. Babies with the medical condition would be the wrong choice, because you're not a doctor. Right?"

"That's right." Amy said. "I can only teach the stuff that I know works in general with most babies."

"Another way to know that something is the wrong choice is if you don't think it would be valuable to the market. Like, the buyers don't want it." Tom suggested. "I mean, you can't know for sure, but you can probably make a decent guess, right?"

"Yeah, I think so." Amy nodded. "So if I cross out the wrong options, how do I choose from what's left? Do I just flip a coin, or roll some dice?"

"I think there's a better way." Tamara suggested. "Because you're on a tight deadline. So if you're choosing between different options that you know aren't wrong, I think you should always choose the option that will be easiest and fastest for you to put together. At least as a starting point, since you have to get this done as quickly as possible."

"That makes sense. So choosing between focusing on the first month or the first six months, I should go for the first month, because that's less to cover and I can get it done faster. Right?" Amy asked. When her friends nodded, she continued. "And choosing whether it's for mom or for dad, I should go with for mom, because I know that perspective better and I could write it faster?"

"Yeah, exactly." Devi said. "Amy, you've got this. It's going to be hard, but you've totally got this. Just make a list of everything you need to decide, choose something for each of them, and then get to work."

"I can do that." Amy said.

"But first you've got to talk to Mark, right?" Tamara reminder her.

"Yeah, first I have to talk to Mark." Amy said with resolve. Amy looked around at her friends, and smiled with appreciation. Then she noticed for the first time that the meal was done, and the servers were clearing their plates. "Guys, I'm sorry, I've monopolized the whole conversation!"

"Don't worry about it, hon. We can do updates quickly over dessert." Tamara said, giving Amy's arm a squeeze. "This is what we're all here for, right?"

"It sure is." Tom said firmly, but with a smile.

Chapter 9
COMING CLEAN

After leaving the restaurant, Amy drove to the beach. She parked her car, got out, and went for a long walk. She thought about the best way to tell Mark what had happened, and how she would explain what she was planning to do. She imagined different ways the conversation might go, and thought about how she would respond to different questions that he might ask.

After hours of walking, she felt ready. She returned to her car and drove back to the apartment, knowing exactly how she would start this difficult conversation. She walked in the door, and could sense that Mark was already home.

"Hi Mark, I'm home." Amy called out.

"I'm in the kitchen." Mark called back. Amy could tell from his voice that something was wrong.

She walked to the kitchen, and saw him sitting at the table, in front of the credit card bill that she had left there earlier that day. Her heart sank – so much for her carefully laid plan.

"Amy, what's this about?" Mark asked, gesturing to the bill.

Mark listened quietly while Amy told him the whole story. When she was done, there was a long pause. Amy could tell from Mark's face that he was upset, and that he wasn't ready to talk about it yet.

"I need to think about this. I'm going to take a shower." Mark said. He slowly got up and walked out of the kitchen, leaving Amy alone with her thoughts.

Chapter 10
THE CHALLENGE

D inner that night was tense. Amy could tell that Mark wasn't ready to talk yet, and anyway in front of the kids wasn't the place to have this conversation. So Amy tried to chat with the kids, but that didn't go very far either. Rick was in one of his teenager moods and didn't want to engage beyond a few sentences about a computer art project of his. So they listened to Daisy's stories about her school friends, punctuated by the occasional snide comment from her brother, which quickly devolved into full-scale bickering about having to share a room. This just made Amy feel even more guilty about their cramped living quarters, so they finished dinner in tense silence.

After dinner the kids went to their shared room to do homework, each with headphones on to block out sounds of the other. Amy and Mark cleared the table. Mark rinsed the plates, and handed them to Amy to load into the dishwasher.

They worked in silence, until a moment broke the tension.

Mark handed Amy a plastic plate, and without thinking she put it on the lower shelf. Turning to take the next plate, she caught an annoyed look in his eye.

Really? He wants to have the dishwasher fight now?!

Mark didn't say anything, but the look was enough.

"Oh, come on. Give me a break – everything doesn't have to be so controlled all the time. So what if the dish is in the bottom shelf?" Amy exploded.

"It's not where they go!" Mark shouted back. "They don't clean properly. When I take the dishes out in the morning, they're still dirty. You can't be so cavalier about everything."

Amy was ready with an angry response, but paused for just a moment as their eyes met. An entire conversation transpired in an instant, the way it only can with two people who've known and loved each other for decades.

"I think this isn't just about the dishwasher." Amy admitted.

"No, you're right, it isn't." Mark agreed. "I'm sorry I shouted."

"Me too." Amy said, reaching back into the dishwasher and moving the plate as a gesture of appeasement.

They finished cleaning up, and sat down to talk. Finally, Amy could say the things that she had planned at the beach.

"Look, Mark, I'm really sorry. Truly." She began. "I know I let you down. It was a stupid mistake. And I know I only have a month left. But I think I can make this work, I really do."

"Amy, it's not about the deadline. We just can't keep going like this forever." Mark said, gesturing at their cramped living quarters. "And I know how much this means to you. Making this work for yourself, and also being there for your dad. I think it's so important that you've been able to do that this year."

Amy felt a wave of emotion thinking about her dad.

"It's been really great to spend that time with him. I think he needed it, but I needed it too. We've gotten closer this year. It's been really special." Amy said. "Thank you for being onboard with doing it."

"Of course, Amy, come on, it's your dad." Mark said. "And look, I really don't care about the deadline. We just can't go on like this forever. You've got an idea that you believe in, right?"

Amy nodded. "Yes, I really do."

"Then look, let's not rush this. How long do you really think you need to do it right, and figure this out?" Mark asked.

"Honestly, I don't know." Amy replied. "Maybe a few months? That will be enough time to figure things out, but not so much that the pressure lets up. A bit of pressure would be good right now."

"So how about this." Mark suggested. "Let's go all in. You lost about five thousand dollars, so what if we make that the bar for keeping this going. You have three months to make back five thousand dollars. If you do it, then you keep on going, because we know that this has really got legs. And if not, then we wave the white flag. How does that sound?"

"Five thousand dollars in three months?" Amy asked, thinking it over. "That sounds like a challenge."

"Yeah?" Mark asked, prodding.

"Yeah. A good challenge." Amy continued. "Yes, I like it. That's more than fair."

"Cool. Should we make it interesting?" Mark asked, a twinkle in his eye.

"It isn't interesting already?" Amy asked.

"Well, sure it is." Mark said. "But for just a little extra incentive, how about this: if you make back the five thousand dollars in the next three months, I'll do all the dishes for a year. And I might even put the occasional plastic dish on the bottom shelf."

"That sounds like you're betting against me!" Amy said, making a face.

"No, just adding some extra motivation. If you don't manage it, we'll just make the kids do the dishes." He added with a smile.

"Haha, fair enough. Okay, you're on." Amy said with a grin. "You're right, now I'm extra motivated! Mark, seriously, thank you for being so supportive with this."

"I don't have a choice, it's in the vows." Mark replied. "Hey, listen, here's a thought. You want to give this all you've got, right?"

"Yeah, for sure." Amy said.

"Well, I know you're getting advice from your mastermind group, but none of you have figured this out yet. Shouldn't you get some guidance from someone who knows what he's doing?" Mark asked.

"Sure," Amy replied, "but who would I ask?"

"What about that guy Kevin, who rear-ended your car. Isn't this what he does for a living?" Mark asked.

"You're right, it is." Amy nodded. "I totally forgot. But it's his work, I feel bad asking."

"Amy, come on. He rear-ended your car. And you helped with his baby." Mark said with just a hint of exasperation. "You said you want to give this all you've got."

"You're right, I do." Amy conceded. "All right, I'll do it. I'll reach out to him tomorrow."

Chapter 11
ASKING FOR HELP

The next morning, Amy felt the urge to tidy. She put things away, washed dishes by hand, and vacuumed the apartment. She was self-aware enough to recognize what was going on.

I'm procrastinating.

Amy knew that she was avoiding the item listed at the top of her to-do list: Call Kevin.

I don't know why I feel so uncomfortable, but I do.

Amy had never liked asking for help. Ever since she was a child, she had wanted to be independent, and take care of things for herself. That was a big part of what made her so uncomfortable about this last year of trying to figure out her business while Mark took care of the bills. It felt a bit too much like a throwback to traditional gender roles.

It's funny, because I know Mark doesn't see it that way.

Mark had made it clear on several occasions that this was just what the startup phase of a business was supposed to look like. And he reminded her that she had picked up the slack financially when they had just married and he was finishing law school.

But this felt different to her. Law school hadn't felt like a gamble, like something that he was doing on a lark. Starting a business felt vague and amorphous, to the point of bordering on self-indulgent.

I mean, who am I to be doing all this?

That was the real question that nagged at the back of Amy's mind. Who was she to do this? Why wasn't she satisfied with the same life that millions of people across the country were living? What entitled her to more?

But she did have that feeling. That there could and should be more to life. That there must be a way to do meaningful work and make a good living and also have the freedom to be there for the people she cared about.

She felt it strongly enough to have spent the last year working on her business – strongly enough to keep going even when she hit a road block or snagged in a pot hole, to the tune of thousands of dollars lost on Facebook.

But the uncertainty nagged at her, and it came to a head when she had to face other people, and ask for their help.

That's what I'm really scared of. That Kevin will say that my idea is stupid or that I don't have what it takes. Or that even if he's too polite to say it, that's what he'll think.

Amy sighed.

Okay, I know that these fears aren't just going to go away.

It's time to put up or shut up.

Amy reached for her phone.

Let's just get this over with.

Amy found Kevin in her contacts, and started the call.

"Amy!" Kevin's voice came through the phone.

"Hi Kevin." Amy said. "How are you doing? How are Alyssa and Liam?"

"We're great." Kevin replied warmly. "Liam is sleeping, which means Alyssa and I are sleeping. Which means everyone is happier. How about you? How are you and Mark and the kids?"

"We're good." Amy replied. She took a deep breath, and continued. "There's actually something that I was hoping you could help me with."

"Oh? What's that?" Kevin asked.

"Well, I'm not sure if you remember, but I'm trying to build this online business." Amy began.

"Sure I do." Kevin replied. "What's up?"

"I guess I could use some input. Any chance that I could run my plan by you, and get some feedback?" Amy asked.

"Of course, I'd be happy to!" Kevin said. "Want to meet at Café Java tomorrow morning, say around ten?"

Chapter 12
GETTING SERIOUS

The next morning, Amy was sitting in a booth at Café Java – as luck would have it, the same booth where she had met Kevin the last time. She had again arrived early, and was nursing her tea when Kevin arrived. He waved at her and came over.

"Good morning!" He said.

"Good morning." Amy replied. "You're in a good mood!"

"I've been in a good mood for the last month, since Liam started sleeping." Kevin said. "Thanks to you."

Kevin ordered a cup of coffee, and they got right down to business.

"So what's going on?" He asked. "What can I help you with?"

Amy spent the next twenty minutes bringing Kevin up to speed on the whole project; why she cared about doing this in the first place, what the last year had been like, the mistake with

Facebook, and the plan for the Baby Manual. When she was done, there was a long pause as Kevin collected his thoughts.

"So, what do you think?" Amy prodded gently.

"Amy," Kevin began, and then paused. A moment later, he continued, "how much help are you looking for here? Do you just want a few tips, or do you really want my help to make this work?"

Amy paused. She didn't know what Kevin charged his clients, but she could guess from his house and his car that it was a lot. "Kevin, I don't think I could afford to hire you—"

Kevin interrupted her. "No, no, that's not what I meant. Amy, Alyssa and I are super grateful to you, and I'd love to help you. You don't need to pay me."

"Thank you, Kevin, that's very kind of you." Amy said.

"Of course, you're welcome." Kevin said, and then continued. "What I meant is that this is what I do for a living, and when people do hire me they expect me to give them the whole truth about what will and won't work, and what it will take for them to build something real. But when friends ask me for advice, sometimes they just want a pat on the back, and when I give them real feedback they end up getting upset. That's the last thing I'd want to happen with you. So if you really want my help to make this work, I'm absolutely in. But if you're committed to proceeding the way you just described and you don't want me to say things that you don't want to hear, I need to know that now."

"I understand." Amy nodded. "I want you to help me. I need to make this work. If I'm making a mistake, it might not be pleasant to learn that, but I need to know."

"All right." Kevin said. "In that case, I have good news and bad news. Which do you want first?"

"The bad news?" Amy asked.

"Everyone goes for the bad news first." Kevin said with a wink. "Actually, let me start with the good news: I do think you can make this business work, and earn the five thousand dollars that you need in the next three months. It probably won't even take that long."

Amy smiled with relief. "So what's the bad news?"

"The bad news is that I don't think you can do it with the Baby Manual." Kevin said, and waited a moment for Amy to absorb what he had told her.

"What do you mean?" She asked.

"Part of it is that I'm not wild about the promise. There are lots of books out there that talk about everything relating to your new baby. I know, because I read a few of them, and they didn't help all that much. There's a risk of being a mile wide and an inch deep with something like this, and even if you aren't there's a risk of being perceived that way." Kevin explained.

"I have been struggling to figure out what to include and what to leave out." Amy admitted.

"Right." Kevin continued. "But the biggest issue is the perceived and actual value of the format. Books and manuals are usually perceived as relatively low value, because we all know what a book is 'supposed' to cost. Twenty or thirty bucks." Kevin began.

"But that's what I was thinking to charge, twenty-seven dollars." Amy explained.

"Okay, so let's do the math. For you to hit your five-thousand-dollar target, you'll need to sell almost two hundred books, right?" Kevin asked. Amy nodded, so Kevin continued. "Not everyone that you tell about the book will end up buying it – let's say that one in five people you present the offer to end up taking it."

"Only one in five?" Amy asked. "Isn't that pretty bad?"

"No, that would actually be pretty good. But really, it depends on how you approach them. If these are people who already know and trust you and you talk to them one on one, it might be realistic. But that would mean you'd need to have a thousand conversations in the next three months. That just isn't practical, is it?" Amy agreed that it wasn't, so Kevin continued his explanation. "On the other hand, if you're reaching strangers through ads on Facebook, it's a wildly optimistic number. One in fifty is probably more like it."

"Which means I'd have to reach ten thousand people with the ads?" Amy asked.

"Exactly. And then you have the cost of the ads to consider. Even if you could get a lead for just one dollar – which is unlikely – you'd be spending two dollars for every dollar that you earn. So the math doesn't work."

"I don't get it – there are tons of things out there being sold for twenty or thirty bucks. How do they make the math work?" Amy asked.

"You're right, but they generally have an unfair advantage working in their favor. They either already have access to a big audience, so they don't have to pay to get their customers one by one. Or they have a catalog of products. So it's okay if they lose money on the first sale, because they know they make up for it down the line. Does that make sense?" Kevin asked.

"I think so." Amy replied. "Kind of like the phone companies can lose money giving me a nice phone if I sign up for a plan, because they know they'll make money over time."

"Yes, exactly." Kevin nodded.

Amy was clearly discouraged. "But you said there was good news, that you think I can make this work. How would I do that?"

"I do think you can make this work. You'd have to sell something more expensive, though." Kevin answered.

"How much more expensive?" Amy asked.

"That depends on what we end up making the product, but at least a few hundred dollars, and maybe more." Kevin replied.

"A few hundred dollars? How could I charge that much?" Amy asked.

"Amy, you could have charged me a few hundred dollars for helping with Liam, and I wouldn't have batted an eye. That's actually what I was expecting." Kevin told her.

"For a bit of advice?" Amy asked again, incredulous.

"No, for helping me solve a really serious problem." Kevin explained. "When people have serious problems, they spend serious money solving them. How much money do you think new parents spend on lactation consultants, sleep specialists, and gear that they don't need? How much money do you think they spend over the first few years of the kid's life on learning and parenting specialists, and even marriage counseling because of the strain that the kid puts on their relationship?"

"But most people don't do any of that." Amy answered.

"I don't know if *most* people do or don't, but that doesn't really matter. What matters is what *some* people do. The people who care enough about these problems." Kevin replied. "You don't want to create a product that would be sort of interesting to everyone, you want to create a product that is absolutely needed by a much smaller group of people. Speaking for myself, I wouldn't pay twenty seven dollars for a baby manual that I might not even have time to read, but I definitely would have paid someone who had the key to making Liam sleep!"

"So are you saying that should be my product? A guide to getting babies to sleep?" Amy asked.

"Don't worry about the format for now, we can work that out a bit later. Right now you need to figure out what the focus of the product will be. And it could be the sleep thing, but we don't know that yet." Kevin explained.

"I don't understand." Amy said. "What are we waiting for?"

"Well, we already have some reasons to believe that the sleep angle will be successful, because you've had people approach you about this dozens of times over the years. And there's my experience." Kevin added, gesturing at himself. "And there's just common sense – we know that every new parent is sleep deprived, and that not sleeping is a killer. So we have some good hunches. But we need to do some actual market research."

"You mean like looking at census data, that sort of thing?" Amy asked, confused.

"Well, occasionally something like that ends up being helpful," Kevin began, "but usually the market research that I recommend is much more practical. I want you to find a few dozen new moms, and find out what their biggest challenges are right now."

"Won't that take a lot of time?" Amy asked. "I feel like with such a tight deadline, I need to move faster than that."

"Amy, there's an old Gandhi quote, that 'it doesn't matter how fast you're moving if you're headed in the wrong direction'." Amy nodded, conceding the point, so Kevin continued. "But look, how long does it really need to take for you to talk to a few dozen women? Maybe a couple of weeks?"

"You're right, I can make that happen. And I can probably get some people to help me, too." Amy added.

"For sure. I know that Alyssa is in a bunch of these mom groups, I'm sure she'd be happy to help." Kevin suggested.

"Okay, got it. I can do that." Amy said firmly. "What do I need to ask them?"

"Well, you need to find language that works with your style, so it doesn't feel like you're reading off of a script." Kevin explained. "But fundamentally, you want to find out what they would want help with if they were sitting down with an expert like you. And a good follow-up question is what they've already tried to solve the problem, and how much money they've spent."

"Would people feel comfortable just telling me those things?" Amy asked.

"If you tell them that you're doing research, then yeah, I think they will." Kevin said, nodding.

"Okay, got it." Amy said.

"Great. So how about this. You do the research, and we'll meet again in a couple of weeks to go over what you've found?"

"That sounds great." Amy said with a smile. "I really feel like I can do this."

Chapter 13
GAME PLAN

Amy knew that she would need help to get the research done – both practically, and in terms of moral support. She planned to enlist her entire family, and that night was the perfect opportunity: family dinner at her father's house.

They all arrived, and had a nice evening chatting and catching up over fresh tacos that Rosa had prepared. After dinner, Amy steeled herself before standing up and addressing the table.

"Guys, there's something that I want to tell you about, and that I need your help with." She began. Everyone was silent, waiting for her to continue. She took a deep breath, and brought everyone up to speed about her business, the advice that Kevin had given her, and the research that she had to do.

"I'm going to need help doing all this." She explained.

"Of course, honey." Amy's father was the first to reply, and the others nodded in agreement. "What do you need?"

"Two things." Amy explained. "First, I need help thinking through exactly how I'm going to do the research. And second, I think I need help talking to people, so that we get enough information back in time."

"Okay. Let's talk about the research first." Mark suggested. "What are we trying to find out?"

"The way Kevin explained it, we want to ask what they would want to know if they were sitting down with an expert on babies and parenting. And he said that a good follow-up question is what they've already tried to solve the problem they bring up, and how much money they've spent." Amy answered. "But I was wondering if maybe we should make a list of things that they might want, and ask people to rate them?"

"No, I think I understand the logic behind the structure that Kevin suggested." Mark replied thoughtfully. "By just asking what they'd want to talk about, and not suggesting topics, you're being careful not to lead the witness. So you're not planting ideas in their head that weren't already there. That would be important, for the results of the research to be useful."

"Oh, that makes sense." Amy said, nodding.

"So I guess that means we have to just talk to them and have a conversation, and write down our notes about what they said afterwards." Mark continued, and then added. "We have to be careful to write down their exact words for how they're describing the problem, so we know how they think about it. We shouldn't be paraphrasing."

"Yup, good point." Amy agreed.

"What about getting their contact information?" David asked. "You know, so we can follow up with them later."

Rick looked up from his phone for the first time in the conversation. He looked annoyed. "Aren't surveys supposed to be anonymous?" He asked.

"Sometimes, but not always." David replied. "And if you make something based on what they tell you they need, don't you think they'd want to know about it? And wouldn't you want to be able to tell them, since they could be great customers for you?"

"I don't know, dad." Amy replied. "I don't want them to feel uncomfortable."

"Why not just give them the option at the end?" Mark suggested. "So when you're done asking them other things, you can say something like 'If we end up making something to help with this, would you want us to tell you about it?' Would that work?" Amy nodded.

"Okay, so we want to reach new parents, right? That's who we should be interviewing?" David asked.

"Yes, that's right." Amy said.

"Okay, so we need to figure out how to reach them." David said, his sales executive instincts kicking into full gear. "And who's going to do the outreach? Amy, do you have people that you can talk to?"

"No, I don't think so. The people we know have kids that are older." Amy said.

"Yeah, but they might know other people." Mark suggested. "I think you need to get in touch with everyone you know, tell them about the research you're doing, and ask who they can connect you with. Lots of people know new parents."

Amy paused for a moment. The prospect of reaching out to people to ask for favors seemed daunting. But looking around the room at the entire family mobilizing to help her, she could hardly say no. "Yes, you're right. I can do that. And Kevin mentioned that his wife Alyssa could talk to women in the mom groups that she's a part of. I'll reach out and talk to her, too."

"I can talk to people at the breastfeeding clinic at the hospital." Rosa suggested. "There are lots of new moms there, and they're usually pretty chatty."

"I have an idea." Twelve-year-old Daisy said, raising her hand.

"What is it, honey?" Amy asked.

"I can talk to Mrs. Harrison, who lives next door to grandpa." Daisy offered. "She just had a baby, and I help sometimes with her garden. I can go talk to her right now."

"That's a great idea, honey, go ahead." Mark said.

"What a go getter!" David said approvingly, as Daisy headed to the door.

"Okay, I can't be one-upped by my daughter!" Mark said with a grin. "I can talk to people at the nursery on the bottom floor of my office building."

"I can reach out to my friends, and see if any of their kids or grandkids might be good fits." David offered.

There was a pause, as eyes turned to Rick. He looked up from his phone as he realized that everyone was looking at him. "I don't know anyone who's having babies." He mumbled. "I can't help with this."

Is he upset about something, or is he just being a teenager?

Amy didn't want to fight in front of the whole family. "That's okay, honey." She said.

"Okay everybody, what's our goal?" David asked.

"What do you mean?" Amy asked.

"Everyone should have a target of how many conversations they're going to have, so we can be sure you get enough useful information back." David explained.

"Well, I'll reach out to everyone that I know. Maybe I'll get connected with five or ten people?" Amy asked.

"How about if you keep pushing until you've at least gotten ten?" David suggested with a grin.

"Okay dad, fair enough." Amy nodded.

"Rosa, Mark, what about you?" David asked?

"There are lots of women coming through the breast-feeding clinic. I should be able to talk to twenty, no problem." Rosa offered.

"And I can probably get ten as well." Mark said.

"Great. I'll lean on my friends to get us at least five more." David said with a smile. "And let's say that Kevin's wife does another five on top of that. So that brings us to fifty conversations. Fifty-one with the one Daisy's doing right now."

"That would be great." Amy said. "Guys, I really appreciate all of you helping with this!"

"We're all here for you, honey. That's what family is for." Mark said, and the others nodded. Except for Rick, who was glaring at Amy.

"We need a deadline." David told the group, oblivious to his grandson's worsening mood. "How about if we get this all done in the next two weeks?"

Everybody nodded, except Rick.

"So everyone is jumping on this? Is that what's going on?" Rick shouted.

"Son, what's wrong?" Mark asked him.

"This is just another one of mom's schemes, that she's been chasing all year. And it isn't helping the family, it's just making things worse." Rick paused, his eyes fixating on his mom. "I saw the credit card bill, mom. I know what you did."

Amy was taken aback. She was about to speak, when Daisy walked back in the door.

"How did it go, kiddo?" David asked her, trying to change the subject and diffuse the tension.

"Great. Mrs. Harrison had a lot to share, and it was fun talking to her." Daisy said with a smile.

"I can't believe you guys!" Rick shouted. "How are you all falling for this again?" He got up and stomped out of the living room.

"All right, that's enough." Mark said, getting up to follow his son.

"No, Mark," Amy gestured for him to sit down, "I'll talk to him." She got up to go after him.

As she walked out of the room, David turned to his granddaughter. "You should write down what Mrs. Harrison told you, before you forget." David suggested.

"Oh, no need. I just recorded the conversation on my phone. She was fine with it." Daisy said.

"Hah, I didn't even think of that." David smiled. "Everyone, if people are comfortable I guess that's also an option."

Chapter 14

RICK

When Amy walked out of the room, she paused for a moment to collect her thoughts. Then, she followed Rick to her father's home office. She found Rick sitting behind the desk, hunched over and staring at his phone. Amy knocked gently on the door, but Rick didn't move – making a point of ignoring her.

"You know, this used to be my room." Amy said. "When I went away to college, your grandparents didn't change a thing. It was only after I graduated and stayed in Ohio with your dad that they turned this into an office. And the first time I came back to visit after that, it was the strangest thing – it felt like a piece of my childhood was gone. But that's how life goes, Rick. Things change, and we can't stay stuck on the way things used to be. There's a whole new phase of life ahead of us to experience. I know that things were good in Ohio, but we had to move out here. Would you really want us to have stayed away from your grandfather, when he was going through all this?"

"Oh, mom, come on!" Rick answered, putting down his phone. "Of course I'm glad that we're closer to grandpa. You know that's not what this is about."

"I don't know, Rick." Amy told her son. "What is it about then?"

"You used to have a job when we were in Ohio. We used to be able to afford things." Rick paused, and then continued. "Mom, I remember when I was younger, we were having a fight about doing my homework, and you told me that our family is a team. That it's mine and Daisy's job to do our schoolwork and chores, and it's yours and dad's job to go to work and make a living. You haven't been doing that, you just haven't. You're the one who's letting us down."

Amy winced at her son's words, because they echoed too closely to the insecurities that she was already feeling. But he wasn't done.

"And I saw the credit card bill, you left it on the table." Rick continued. "It's not enough that you're not doing your job, you're spending all this money on your projects that aren't going anywhere."

"That's what you're mad about?" Amy asked softly.

"Yes, that's what I'm mad about!" Rick shouted. It dawned on Amy that Rick's frustration must have been simmering for a while. "And now you're doing it again, and nobody seems to notice. You're taking the whole family for a ride, and none of them can see that you're conning us."

"Rick, watch your tone." Amy said, a little angry and very hurt. "I understand that you're mad, and I want to talk about it. But I'm still your mother."

"Fine." Rick grunted. "I'm sorry."

"Rick, you're right that I haven't been pulling my weight." Amy said. "I talked about this with your dad when we moved here... maybe we should have all talked as a family. I don't want to waste our money, or make things harder. But I also don't want to just find a job that keeps me busy and away from your grandfather all day, doing something that I don't really care about. I had a deal with your dad, that I would take a year to try to figure this out. And I'm almost out of time."

"How does spending five thousand dollars on Facebook help with that?" Rick asked, still defiant.

"It doesn't, Rick." Amy sighed. "I mean, it was supposed to. I was running a small test with a few hundred dollars to see if I could sell this smoothie product. But I messed up. It wasn't setup properly, and I forgot to turn it off, so all that money got spent. I feel terrible about it."

Rick could see that his mother was telling the truth, and his glare began to soften.

"You know, Rick," Amy said with emotion, "I wonder sometimes if I should quit. Just give up and go get a job, like I had in Ohio. I think about that a lot, actually. But you know why I haven't done it?"

"No, why?" Rick asked.

"Because of you, Rick." Amy answered. "You and Daisy. I wanted to show you that if you want to do more than everyone else around you is doing, you could take a chance and try to make that happen. But maybe I'm just kidding myself..."

Amy turned away, to wipe a tear from her eye.

"Mom," Rick began, "I'm sorry."

"It's okay. I'm all right." Amy said.

Rick paused. Until that moment, it hadn't occurred to him that things had been hard for her, too.

"You're really doing this for us?" Rick asked.

"Yes, of course I am." Amy answered. "But I know it's been hard. Maybe I didn't realize how hard it's been. Maybe I should have talked to you more about what I'm doing, and why I care about this. I'm sorry, I really am. And this really is the last chance. If I can't make it work this time, then I'm going to give up and get a job. That's why I need everyone's support to make it work."

Rick was quiet. Being a teenager, his focus hadn't extended beyond his own experience. Amy was his mother – he had just assumed that she had it all together. He was realizing for the first time that this had been difficult for her, too. And that he had probably been making it worse.

After a few moments of silence, Amy continued. "Rick, it's okay. I understand if you don't support this. Hopefully it will work out, but even if it doesn't it's going to be over soon."

She turned to leave, disappointed, but Rick stopped her.

"Mom, wait." He said. "I'm sorry. I didn't realize that things were hard for you, too. And I didn't mean to make it worse."

"Thank you, honey." Amy said. "I just need you to give me the benefit of the doubt for a little while longer. Can you do that?"

"Yeah, mom, I can." Rick agreed.

Chapter 15
RESULTS

A couple of weeks later, the whole family (plus Rosa) was gathered in David's living room.

"Everyone, I want to say how much I appreciate all of you digging in over the last couple of weeks to help with the research for my program." Amy began. "I know you've all been hustling, and it means a lot to me."

"Of course we're in your corner, honey." Mark said.

"For sure, mom." Daisy added. "And it was kind of fun."

"So, how did we do?" David asked.

"Everyone did really well." Amy replied. "Rick, can you break it down for us?"

"Sure thing, mom." Rick replied. As a peace offering after their last conversation, he had volunteered to tabulate all the responses that the group had collected. He opened his laptop and shared the results. "Okay, so our best performer by far was Rosa. She got twenty-nine responses."

"It helps that there are so many women coming through the breastfeeding clinic, who are starved for conversations with an adult." Rosa said with a grin.

"Well, it's still a great number." Rick replied. "And in second place was mom. She was a rock star – she got twenty-four responses."

"That's great, honey." David said approvingly. "This was all from calling your friends?"

"Yeah." Amy replied. "The first few calls were pretty uncomfortable, but once I got into the swing of things it was fun. I got to catch up with a lot of people that I haven't talked to since we left Ohio, and even some people here that I hadn't connected with since I left for college."

"That does sound fun." Rosa said. "So you found twenty-four people who you know who all had babies?"

"No, no. Just a few." Amy explained. "But I didn't just ask if they had a newborn, I also asked if they know anyone who did, and that opened a lot more doors."

"And you thought you wouldn't even get to ten!" David reminded her.

"You were right, dad. Thanks for pushing me." Amy said.

"Anytime, hon. That's my job." David replied.

"Well, good job mom." Rick said. "Next up is Alyssa. She got sixteen."

"That's your friend Kevin's wife?" Rosa asked.

"Yeah, that's right. She was great, and I guess it helps that she's got a baby herself, so she's plugged in with all the mom groups in town." Amy explained.

"Okay. Next is dad." Rick continued. "Dad got eight."

"I think I'm the only one who missed the target." Mark said ruefully. "I'm sorry, honey. It was a busy couple of weeks at the office, and I couldn't get away for too long."

"It's fine, honey." Amy replied. "I really appreciate it."

"Next up is grandpa." Rick continued. "He got five."

"I had to fight for them, too." David said ruefully. "I made a lot of calls, but everyone I know either has kids too old, or grandkids too young. But I kept on pushing to get to five. That's why we have quotas."

"We appreciate it, David." Mark said.

"What about me?" Daisy asked.

"What about you, sweetie?" Mark asked.

"She got three." Rick answered.

"That's right. I asked my friends at school if they knew anyone who had a baby at home, and tracked down a couple more people." Daisy explained.

"Nice work, kiddo." David said.

"So all together, we've got eighty-three responses!" Rick exclaimed.

"Wow. That's amazing. Well done, everyone." Amy said.

"Nice!" David added. "So what did we learn?"

"Well," Rick began, "I got everyone's responses and plugged them into a spreadsheet so we could keep track of them. Then I used this word cloud analyzer tool that I found online to pull out the most common keywords and phrases that came up."

"That's pretty neat, son." Mark said approvingly.

"Thanks, dad." Rick nodded. "So anyway, I've got this word cloud that I can show you, but it might be easier if I just read the list of the top keywords. They were 'baby', 'sleep', 'nursing', 'tired', and 'crying. I can keep going down the list if you want."

"No, that's fine Rick, thanks." Amy replied. "We did all this to validate the assumption that people cared about the problem of getting their babies to sleep, and it sounds like the answers are supporting that idea. Right?"

"Yeah, absolutely. It's three of the top five keywords." Rick replied.

"Three?" Daisy asked.

"Yeah, there's 'baby', 'sleep', and 'tired'." Rick explained.

"Oh, right." Daisy said.

"We could even say three and a half." Rosa added. "Since half the time babies are crying, it's when they're tired."

"That's true. So what's the next step?" Mark asked.

"Well, I've already sent Rick's spreadsheet to Kevin, and I'm meeting with him to go over it in the morning." Amy explained. "But it looks like the next step is going to be building a something, like a book or course or something, to help parents get their babies to sleep."

"So you'll make something that teaches other parents?" Daisy asked. "That's really cool, mom."

"What are you going to call it?" Rosa asked.

"What do you mean?" Amy asked.

"Well, you're not going to call it 'Amy's sleep thing', are you?" Rosa teased her friend. "It needs a name."

"How about Night Nurse?" David suggested.

"No, that's something else. A night nurse is someone who comes to live with you and take care of the baby at night, so you can sleep." Rosa explained.

"What about The Sleep Solution?" Mark suggested.

"Hmmmm, maybe." Amy said. "I guess that works, but I don't love it."

"Mom, what about calling it Sleepy Baby?" Rick suggested. "Those are the two most common keywords that people are asking for, and it sounds kinda cute."

"Sleepy Baby?" Amy said, listening for how the words sounded out of her mouth. "Sleepy Baby. I like it."

"Well, then here's to Sleepy Baby." David said, raising his glass of water in the gesture of a toast.

"To Sleepy Baby!" Everyone replied.

Chapter 16
PILOT

The next morning, Amy arrived at Café Java and saw that Kevin was already there. He had a cup of coffee and was talking on his cell phone, and there was a hot cup of tea waiting for Amy. She walked over to the table, and Kevin gestured for her to sit down.

"Listen, I have to go. Let's finish this conversation later, okay?" Kevin said to wrap up his call. He put away the phone and smiled at Amy. "Good morning."

"Good morning!" She replied.

"I looked at your research results last night. It looks promising." Kevin said.

"It really does." Amy said, excited. "It seems like people really do want help getting their babies to sleep. You were right – we probably could have skipped doing the research!"

"Oh, no, I don't agree with that." Kevin replied. "Not about what people want, I agree that they seem to want help getting their babies to sleep. That isn't surprising to me, given the last few months! But I don't think we could have skipped the research. It's really important for us to have spent these last couple of weeks validating our assumptions, so that we can proceed with confidence. That's a lot better than rushing ahead, and then when something goes wrong you don't know what the problem was."

"Okay, that makes sense." Amy nodded.

"Besides," Kevin added, "the research isn't only about validating demand, it's also about learning the language that people use to describe what they're feeling, and what they want. You've got a treasure trove of information here, that will be really helpful as you design your offer and create all the sales materials."

"So does that mean we're ready to build something?" Amy asked.

"Yes, I think so." Kevin replied. "And I think the format that makes sense is an online course that people could access on demand, with very short video lessons teaching each of the parts of your formula. That way busy parents can watch it in pieces, between diaper changes and whatnot." He added with a wink.

"Yeah, that makes sense." Amy nodded.

"I also think it's important for there to be a certain amount of coaching support with you." Kevin continued. "Both to help people get the result, and also to differentiate your offer from the other options that they can choose from."

"What do you mean?" Amy asked.

"Well, there are a lot of books and resources about

getting kids to sleep, but they don't show you what things should look like, and they definitely don't tell you if you're doing it properly. I mean, I'd rather have someone show me exactly how to swaddle a baby in a video than read instructions about how to do it." Kevin explained. "And it would be even better if after they set things up, they can take a photo of the baby's room and send it to you to give them feedback. Or even a before and an after, so they can send you a photo when they join the course, you give them feedback, and then they send you another photo after they make changes."

"That would be pretty easy for me to do." Amy agreed.

"Right," Kevin agreed, "and it's super valuable, and really sets you apart from other options that are just one-way information. You could also give them an 'SOS call' option, where they have one opportunity to get on a call with you during their first month, if they're really losing their minds."

"Couldn't that add up to a lot of calls?" Amy asked.

"Well, it would only be during business hours, and they'd have to reach out to set it up. So it's not like your phone will just randomly be ringing in the middle of the night." Kevin explained. "And not everyone will take you up on the call. But a lot of people will feel very reassured that they can if they need to. Think about it – I mean, for myself, a few months ago when I wasn't sleeping and was basically going insane. Knowing that I could call an expert if I needed to would have been a lifeline."

"You really think people will care that much?" Amy asked.

"Yeah, I really do." Kevin nodded. "Let's say that half

of the people who buy this course end up setting up a call – though I doubt it will be that high. And the calls are half an hour long. So if we sell the course for three hundred dollars, that works out to over a thousand dollars an hour for your time. That's worth it, right?"

"Oh, of course it's worth it. I never would have thought about charging so much. But I guess it makes sense, since it isn't just for the calls, it's also for the whole course." Amy paused. "But isn't it sleazy for me to charge them for these calls if half of the people don't schedule them?"

"Amy, you wouldn't be charging for the calls." Kevin explained. "You would be charging them for the peace of mind of knowing that there's someone in their corner. It's like insurance – as long as the premiums are fair, you shouldn't feel like a sucker because you never make a claim. You probably hope that you *never* have to make a claim."

"Right." Amy nodded. "But you definitely want to have it in case there's a fire or something."

"That, or someone rear-ends your car." Kevin added.

"Haha, right." Amy smiled.

"But it's not even just that." Kevin continued. "They're really paying for the entire package – for their baby to sleep, so that they can sleep. That's what people will pay to get from you."

"Okay, got it. So I guess my next step is to write the scripts, film the videos, and all that stuff?" Amy asked. "Can you help me figure out how to do all that?"

"I can help you figure out how to do all that, when the time comes." Kevin replied. "But that isn't your next step.

You're not ready to build out the full course yet. Right now what you need to do is offer a pilot."

"A pilot?" Amy asked. "Like with TV shows?"

"Yes, exactly." Kevin confirmed. "Just like before they spend the time and money to produce a new TV show they make a pilot, you want to do the same thing with a course. Because even though the research is looking promising and you've got a strong idea for what people want, you don't know for sure – and you can't know for sure until people actually pay you money. So that's the next step."

"I don't understand." Amy said, confused. "Why would people pay me money if I haven't made the course yet?"

"Think of it like buying tickets to a show that doesn't happen until next month, or putting a deposit on a car that isn't available yet." Kevin explained. "What you're going to offer people is a special deal for being one of the charter participants in the very first run of your course. So instead of three hundred dollars, you'll only charge two hundred – that's a third off the price. In exchange, they aren't going to get fancy polished videos, they'll get the minimum viable version. Maybe even have your husband or kids film it on a phone, while you explain each lesson. And later on you can upgrade the course with more polished video, and they'll get a free upgrade to the new version."

"I'm not sure I get it." Amy said. "So I'm selling a course that I haven't even built yet?"

"That's exactly right." Kevin said, nodding. "You'll need to create a high-level outline of what you're going to teach and what will be covered, but that's it. And you tell people that this course is going to be released in three weeks or whatever, and if they want one of the twenty-five charter spots they have to reserve it before the course goes live. And of course, if you run out of spots then they'll have to wait until the next time you do it, at the full price."

"Okay, I think I understand." Amy said. "So what do I need to prepare, in order to be ready to start selling?"

"Not that much, actually. You need a high-level outline of what you'll teach – like one page of bullets." Kevin explained. "And you'll need a simple sales infrastructure – a sales page with basic information about the course, and a way for people to pay."

"Like to accept credit cards?" Amy asked.

"Yes, exactly." Kevin replied, and then continued. "But it doesn't have to be complicated – you can set it up with something like Stripe or PayPal, it's really straight-forward."

"Okay. I should be able to do all that in the next couple of weeks. So after that I start selling?" Amy asked.

"Yes, that's right." Kevin nodded.

"How do I do that? I guess with ads on Facebook?" Amy asked.

"Well, you can try Facebook ads just to see how they perform – as long as it's with a limited and carefully monitored budget." Kevin replied. "But it's usually better to sell your first pilot through one-on-one conversations. You can go back to everyone you spoke with during the research phase, and see if they'd be interested."

There was a pause in the conversation, as Amy considered Kevin's advice. She felt deeply uncomfortable with the idea of sales, and didn't want to appear ungrateful for Kevin's help. But on the other hand, if she didn't bring it up she wouldn't get his input, and she needed all the help that she could get. She decided to bring up her concern.

"Kevin, I'm not sure about that." Amy said diplomatically. "I really don't like hard selling, that's just not who I am."

"Amy, I'm not suggesting any hard selling, but you do have to sell your course." Kevin replied. "Not just because it's the best way to make sales at this stage – which it is – but also because if people don't want it, you need to hear why. That's important information for you to have! But look, this isn't hard selling. You just go back to the people from the research, and tell them that based on their input, you're creating this course – and would they like to hear about it?"

"That's it?" Amy asked.

"Yup, that's it." Kevin explained. "If they say yes – and most people will, just out of curiosity and politeness – then you give them the one-minute explanation of what the course will do for them, and how it works. Then you ask if they might be interested in signing up."

"What if they don't say yes?" Amy asked.

"Well, they definitely won't say yes." Kevin replied.

"What do you mean? Don't I want them to say yes?" Amy asked.

"Sure." Kevin explained. "But they can't say yes after hearing a sixty second description. The best you'll get is a 'maybe, tell me more'. So they might say that, or they might just say no."

"Okay. So what do I do if they say no?" Amy asked. "I

don't want to hard sell them or convince them, that would feel weird."

"I agree, I don't think you should do that. If they say no, just ask them why." Kevin explained. "And make it clear that you're not trying to convince them. But since this is something new that you're creating, you do want their feedback about why they're not interested. Better to find out now than after you've built it, right?"

"Yeah, that makes sense." Amy agreed. "Okay, what if they say maybe?"

"If they say maybe, then you give them all the details – the lesson by lesson breakdown, what the outcomes will be, when the program is going to be released, what's the deadline to sign up, how many people you're accepting into the pilot, what the discounted price is if they join now, and what it will cost if they wait until later." Kevin explained. "Just tell them all the details. And then ask them if they want to sign up."

"Okay, got it." Amy nodded, taking notes.

"Cool." Kevin continued. "And if they say no, it's the same as before – don't try to convince them, just ask for their feedback. But most likely is that they'll say maybe – like that they want to think about it, or talk to their spouse. Those are all different versions of 'maybe'. If they say maybe, then ask if they can give you an answer by a certain deadline."

"I can do that." Amy nodded. "What about if they just say yes?"

"If they say yes, then sign them up!"

"And how do I do that?" Amy asked. "Sign them up, I mean."

"Well, if you're doing these conversations face to face, you could even take cash. But that's probably not how you'll do this." Kevin said. "So your best bet is to have a web page setup that you can point them to."

"So if I call the program Sleepy Baby, then it would be SleepyBaby.com?" Amy asked.

"Yes, exactly." Kevin nodded. "I like the name!"

"Thank you. My son suggested it." Amy said with a smile.

"Smart kid." Kevin grinned. "Okay, so let's talk timelines. You said you think you can get all the setup done in the next couple of weeks?"

"Yeah, I think so." Amy said after a moment. "Rick can help with the website, and my friend Devi is a copywriter, she can help with the sales page."

"Perfect. So send me what you've got in two weeks, and I'll look it over and give you a thumbs up, or feedback if necessary." Kevin suggested. "Actually, that timing works out well – I'm going on a business trip to Gold Lake in Colorado right after that, and the cell reception is usually pretty spotty when I'm up there. So I'll give you feedback before I go, and then I guess you'll be done with the selling by the time I get back."

"That sounds good, Kevin." Amy smiled. "I'm a bit scared, but I really feel like I can do this. Thank you for helping me."

"It's my pleasure, Amy." Kevin said. "And listen, I'm guiding you a bit, but this is all you. Your expertise, your hard work, and ultimately your decisions. You've got this."

Chapter 17

SLEEPLESS

Amy stared at the clock on her nightstand. It was three in the morning, and she was wide awake. It had been just over two weeks since her meeting with Kevin, and in that time she'd been busy. She had worked with Devi to write a sales page for Sleepy Baby, and then with Rick to get the page up on her website and connected to Stripe, so people could pay with a credit card. And while all that was happening, she had created a three page outline of everything that she wanted to cover in her pilot course.

She had spoken to Kevin earlier today (or rather, yesterday). He had given the whole setup a thumbs up before getting on his flight to Denver. All that was left was to start selling, which Amy planned to do first thing in the morning.

She knew that she should try to sleep, but no matter how long she stared at the ceiling, sleep wouldn't come.

This isn't working. I've been awake for two hours, lying here isn't helping!

Amy got out of bed, and walked to the kitchen, carefully closing the bedroom door on her way out so as not to wake Mark. She quietly made herself a cup of chamomile tea.

Come on, Amy. If ever there was a time when you could use a good night's sleep...

For the last two weeks, and especially since her conversation that day with Kevin, Amy oscillated between excitement and fear – sometimes swinging back and forth every few minutes.

This is exciting! I've been working to get here for almost a year, and thinking about it for a lot longer than that. Tomorrow is when it gets real. Finally. Of course I can't sleep!

But that was just half of the story. Because while getting to the end of the road could mean that she was finally arriving at her destination, it could also just mean discovering that the road didn't lead anywhere at all.

And I won't have any excuse, either. We did the research, and Kevin checked it all and signed off. He knows what he's doing. So if this doesn't work, it won't be because of the plan. It'll be because of me.

Amy was so lost in thought that she didn't notice Mark coming out of the bedroom. "Can't sleep?" He asked her.

"No, I'm totally wired." Amy said. "I'm sorry, did I wake you?"

"No, I couldn't sleep either." Mark said, and gestured to Amy's tea. "Give me a sip of that?"

"Sure." Amy said, handing Mark the tea. He took a sip, and handed it back.

"Are you excited about tomorrow?" Mark asked. "Or scared?"

"Both of those things, I think." Amy confessed.

"Yeah, me too." Mark said, putting an arm around his wife.

"I just don't want to disappoint everyone." Amy said with a sigh.

"Honey, you're not going to disappoint anyone." Mark told her.

"You can't know that, Mark." Amy replied. "This might not work."

"I know that, honey." Mark said. "But even if it doesn't work, nobody's going to be disappointed. You're trying to build a business – that means risk and uncertainty. You don't know that it's going to work out. It's not like going to law school – sure, that was hard, but as long as you finish the classes you know that you're going to come out the other end as a lawyer. This is different."

"Yeah, but you knew you had what it takes to be a lawyer." Amy said. "I don't know if I really have what it takes to be an entrepreneur."

"Amy, I know you've got to find this out for yourself, but I am absolutely certain that you have what it takes." Mark told her. "For whatever that's worth."

"It's worth a lot." Amy said. "It really means a lot to me how you've been in my corner this whole time."

Mark shrugged. "It's in the vows, right?"

"Yeah, I guess it is." Amy said with a grin.

"But Amy, seriously, what's really bothering you?" Mark asked again. "There's something specific, isn't there?"

Amy nodded. They'd been married too long for her to hide what was on her mind – not that she wanted to. "It's the selling." She admitted.

"What do you mean?" Mark asked.

"Well, there's a lot about this that feels like a stretch." Amy explained. "I've never put a course together before, creating videos and whatnot feels a bit scary... but I feel like I can do all that. The selling..." Amy's voice trailed off.

"What about it?" Mark asked. "You've sold things before. At the bake sales for the kids' schools, and that telemarketing gig when I was in law school."

"That was awful!" Amy said.

"I know, but I'm saying, you did it. You know how to do it." Mark replied.

"But that was different. There was something that I was selling. Not just a promise that I'll make something if they buy." Amy said. "And I hated the whole thing – calling people, bothering them at home. The guys who were good at that had a knack for sales, they could make everything into a pitch. It was so awkward for me. And this is going to be a hundred times worse."

There was a long pause, as Mark cast about for something comforting to say. He couldn't think of anything, so instead he finally asked, "So what do you want to do about it?"

"What do you mean?" Amy asked. "What can I do about it?"

"Well, you could decide not to do it?" Mark suggested. "I mean, if you don't think it's going to work anyway."

"You know, I thought about it." Amy admitted. "But

Kevin really seems to think that this is the way to go, and I want to give this every chance to succeed."

"Okay, that makes sense." Mark agreed. "And for what it's worth, I don't think it's going to be as bad as you're describing. But listen, you've got your bases covered anyway, right? You're also going to be running the Facebook ads?"

"Yes, I am." Amy answered, and then added. "Carefully – I'll check the budget every day."

"I know, honey. You're not going to make that mistake again." Mark said with a smile.

"No, not when there are so many new mistakes for me to make." Amy said with a wry grin.

"No, you're right. There are lots of new mistakes left to make." Mark agreed with a smile. "And look, we'll get past those mistakes, too. Now come on, let's try to get some sleep. Big day tomorrow."

Amy nodded, and followed her husband back to bed.

Chapter 18

LOCKED OUT

The next morning, Mark and the kids all wished Amy good luck before heading off to work and school. As soon as they were gone, Amy opened up her computer. It was time to turn on the ads. She took a deep breath, and logged into the Facebook ads console – but the screen didn't look the way she expected. She read the message on it, and her eyes widened: "Your account has been disabled. All of your ads have been stopped."

What ads? I wasn't even running any ads!

Amy spent the next hour trying to navigate the ads platform, and researching online to understand what had happened. It took her almost an hour to piece together that Facebook had flagged the VitaMagic Smoothies company for violating their terms of service, and since the ads promoting them were still in her account, it had been shut down.

What am I going to do?

Amy took a deep breath, and tried to regroup. Her first instinct was to grab her sneakers and go for a run, but she knew she didn't have time for that.

Okay, there must be a way to solve this. Kevin will know what to do.

She reached for her phone, and called Kevin – but it went straight to voicemail. She hung up, remembering him saying that he wouldn't have reception on the trip.

Damn it. Damn it!

Next Amy tried calling Mark, but his phone rang until it went to voicemail as well.

"Mark, I know you're in meetings, but I need you to call me when you get this." She spoke into the phone. "My ad account is deactivated. I don't know what to do!"

She hung up, and started pacing.

I can't believe this is happening!

Amy picked up her phone, paused for a moment, and then put it back down.

Okay, I need to talk to someone.

She picked up the phone again, and dialed. Mercifully, the call connected.

"Amy?" Her father's voice came through the phone.

"Dad," she began, "I've got a problem."

Chapter 19
SELLING

Half an hour later, Amy was sitting in her father's living room. It was just her and her dad – Rosa was out running an errand. The whole situation felt a bit comical.

I don't know why I'm here. What's dad going to be able to do? He doesn't know the first thing about Facebook!

But still, she needed to talk to someone, so she explained to her father what had happened, and he did his best to follow the technology parts of it all. He listened patiently, letting her share her frustration with the whole situation. When she was done, he looked at her for a moment before speaking.

"Amy, I don't know anything about Facebook." He began, echoing her thoughts from moments earlier.

"I know, dad." Amy said, starting to stand up. "I'm sorry, I don't know why I'm here."

"Hang on, Amy, sit down. I wasn't done." David interrupted her. She sat back down. "Like I said, I don't know anything about Facebook, but I do know a lot about selling. So what if Facebook isn't working – wasn't that supposed to be your backup plan anyway?"

"Maybe, but it was the only part of the plan that I felt comfortable with!" Amy replied.

"Amy, look – here's what I know." David replied. "Through all that research, we talked to eighty-three people. Sixty-four of them said that if you make something, they'd want to hear about it. So you just need to call them and tell them!"

"Dad, it's not that easy." Amy protested.

"Sure it is. Look, I'll show you right now." David said firmly. Before Amy could protest, he picked up his phone and dialed a number. "Hi, Sharon?" He began. "It's David here. We spoke last week about my daughter, and how she's thinking about making something to help new parents?" He paused, and continued. "I'm good, thanks for asking. And thank you for sharing your perspective with me, it was really helpful. In fact, my daughter decided to create a course to help parents just like you. She's standing right here – would you like to hear about it?" There was a moment's pause, and then answered. "Great. Here you go."

With that, there was a phone in Amy's hand.

"Um, hello?" Amy began.

"Yes, hi." Sharon's voice replied through the phone.

"Um, hi. My name is Amy." Amy began, glaring at her father.

"Talk to her." David whispered insistently. "Tell her about your course."

"Thank you for speaking with me." Amy began, gathering her thoughts and trying to remember Kevin's script. "And thank you for sharing your feedback through my dad. Based on that research, I'm creating an online course that will show parents how to get their babies to sleep. Is... is that something you might be interested in?"

"Hell, yeah!" Sharon replied. "If you can help me get the baby to sleep, I want to hear what you have to say. But I'm so busy with the baby... when are you doing this course?"

"Well, I'm launching it on the twenty-fifth," Amy answered, "but you'll be able to access the videos on demand, so you can go through them whenever you want."

"Tell her about the pictures, and the calls." David whispered.

"Oh, right." Amy continued. "Sharon, the process I teach has a lot to do with the setup of your baby's room, so it's not just a course. You'll also send me a photo of the room so I can give you feedback about what to change, and I'll look at another photo afterwards to make sure you did it right. And if you have questions or something isn't working, you also get a 1-on-1 call with me to help you figure it out."

"Um, it's Amy, right?" Sharon asked.

"Yes, it is." Amy replied.

"Okay. Amy, not to be rude, but how do I know this is going to work? Are you a doctor?" Sharon asked.

"No, I'm not a doctor." Amy answered, her heart sinking.

"Tell her about all the kids you've helped." David whispered to her.

"But I do know what I'm doing." Amy said, nodding

to her dad. "My first baby was a terrible sleeper, so I really had to learn everything about how to get him down. And I just got interested, so I kept on learning about it. He's seventeen now, and over the years I've helped a lot of parents get their babies to sleep."

"Okay, got it." Sharon said. "All right, what's this course going to cost?"

"What's it going to cost? Um, well, I'm thinking, two hundred dollars." Amy said, wincing.

"That's a lot of money." Sharon said. Amy was about to answer, when she heard a sigh through the phone. "Well, I've got to try something – my husband and I are losing our minds. Sure, count us in."

Incredulous, Amy mouthed the words 'she's in!' to her dad.

"Sign her up!" David whispered.

"That's great Sharon, I'm so glad." Amy said. "Shall we get you signed up right now?"

"Sure, but let's do it fast – I think the baby's waking up. This had better work!"

Amy guided Sharon to her website, and walked her through the steps of signing up. She hadn't expected to do it this way, so her explanations were a bit clumsy – but they did the trick. The call wrapped up, and a moment later Amy heard a ding from her phone, indicating a new email: confirmation that her first sale had come through.

Amy sat down on the couch, stunned and exhausted.

"Well, congratulations." David said, smiling.

"Thanks, dad." Amy said after a moment. "I can't believe that happened."

"Was it that bad?" David asked.

"It was terrifying!" Amy answered. "But no, it wasn't that bad."

"Good!" David replied. "Because you're going to have to do a lot more of them!"

"You really think I can do it?" Amy asked.

"You just did it, Amy!" David told his daughter. "Not all that well, but you did it. It's a great start."

"I did make the sale, didn't I?" Amy said. It was just starting to feel real.

"Yes, you did." David replied. "You were lucky that the first call was an easy one, and it closed. They won't all be like that. Some of them will have a lot more questions, and some of them won't want to buy. That's okay – you just keep dialing until you're through the list, and you'll get better at it each time. And I'll be right here."

"Thank you, dad." Amy said. Then she took a deep breath, and picked up the phone.

Chapter 20
LAST DAY

"How are you feeling, dad?" Amy asked.

She was behind the wheel of her car, and her father was in the passenger seat beside her. They had spent the morning at the hospital doing tests, and the doctors were pleased with his progress. Physiotherapy was going well, and they seemed to think that he should be able to continue regaining mobility, and freedom.

"I'm fine, honey." David reassured her. "Just a little tired is all."

"Do you want me to call Mark and tell them to head home?" She asked. The whole family was waiting at David's house, for an impromptu celebration. Today was the last day for people to sign up for the Sleepy Baby course, and they were getting together to check the numbers as a group.

"Of course not! I'm excited to see where you landed!" David said firmly.

When Amy had checked this morning, they were at fourteen sales. She had spoken with Kevin, and he suggested that a bunch of people who were still thinking about the offer would jump in on the last day. But all morning there hadn't been a single ding on her phone, so she was getting herself used to the idea that fourteen was as much as she was going to get. That would still be almost three thousand dollars – a far cry from the five grand that she was aiming for, but a strong indication nonetheless that she was on the right track. But there was no avoiding the truth that Amy wasn't anywhere near her goal. She couldn't help but feeling like, even in relative victory, she had come up short.

Perhaps sensing his daughter's insecurity, David added reassuringly. "And listen, whatever the numbers are, I'm proud of you."

"Thanks, dad." Amy said.

When they arrived at David's house, Mark and the kids were already there, and so was Rosa. They smiled at each other conspiratorially.

"Hi honey, hi David." Mark greeted them. "How did it go today?"

"Well, there was an awful lot of waiting." David answered. "Which is about par for the course at the hospital."

"It went great." Amy interjected. "The doctors are very happy with dad's progress."

"That's great. Way to go, David." Mark said to his father in law.

"So what have you all been up to?" Amy asked.

"Oh, nothing." Daisy said mischievously.

"We were just wondering if you checked your sales today?"

"I checked in the morning, honey." Amy said. "But there haven't been any new sales since then."

"Are you sure about that?" Rick asked. His tone suggested that he knew something that she didn't.

"What's going on?" Amy asked.

"Come here, take a look at this." Mark said, gesturing to the laptop. Amy walked around to look at the screen, and was greeted with a pleasant surprise: the sales tally had jumped to twenty-one.

"How did this happen?" Amy asked.

"We wanted to surprise you, so we got dad to turn off your phone notifications." Rick said with a grin. "And then we called all the people who were still thinking about it, and reminded them that today is their last chance to sign up."

"That's amazing. Thank you!" Amy said.

"We're not quite at the target yet, but we're getting close." Mark said with a smile. "So hopefully a few more come in before the end of the day. In the meantime, we should eat. We got Chinese."

"My favorite." David said appreciatively. "Thanks."

"You bet." Mark said. "It's already on the table. We figured you'd be hungry after all those tests."

"It's not the tests so much as all the waiting in between." David complained. "But yeah, I'm hungry."

The family ate and chatted, but the conversation was subdued. Everyone was anxious about the sales that could still trickle in. Amy's father had a rule that cell phones weren't allowed at the dinner table, and he wasn't willing to make an exception for tonight. So they ate quietly, and every so often Amy thought she heard a ding from her phone – but it was faint enough that she wondered if her mind was playing tricks on her.

Finally, the containers of moo shu pork and Cantonese chow mein began to run low, and Amy couldn't take it any longer.

"I have to check the numbers." She said, and excused herself. But no sooner had she left the room that she came rushing back. "We're at twenty-seven!" She exclaimed. Not only had she met the target, she had exceeded it by two sales!

"That's fantastic!" Mark said.

"Are you going to wait and see how many more will come in?" Rick asked.

"I hadn't thought of that. Honestly, I didn't think we'd even hit the target." Amy paused for a moment, and then continued. "But I told them all that I was only going to have twenty-five people in this first run, so I think we need to shut it down."

"I can redirect the sales page to a waiting list." Rick said as he got up. "Do you want me to refund the last two who signed up?"

"No, let's keep those two." Amy said with a grin. "They did already sign up, after all."

While Rick redirected the page, Amy looked at the sales that had come in on her phone. She was puzzled. "Hang on, there's something weird going on."

"What is it?" Mark asked.

"It's just that there are a few names of people here that I

don't recognize." She explained, counting. "There are four of them. These people weren't a part of our research."

Rick cleared his throat. "Um, mom, I think I know what that's about." He said. "When Alyssa sent me her research conversation information, I noticed that a few of those women mentioned being a part of this online baby forum. So I reached out to them, and asked if they could send a message out to all of their members. They agreed, for a hundred bucks. Dad said it was okay, so I put it on the credit card. The message just went out today."

Amy hugged her son, feeling equal parts gratitude and pride.

"That's so smart!" Rosa said.

"Way to go, kiddo." David said approvingly. "That's what I call initiative!"

They all cheered. Amy had succeeded, and it felt like a team victory – because it was.

"Oh, no." Mark suddenly said.

"What is it? What's wrong?" Amy asked. Had there been a mistake? Was this all some kind of elaborate practical joke?

"Nothing, honey." Mark said. "I just realized that you won the bet. I have to wash the dishes for a year!"

Epilogue

DOING STUFF
THAT MATTERS

Amy smiled as she looked around at her family and friends. Rick was going away to college, and the gang had gathered to give him a proper send-off. A year and a half had passed since the first Sleepy Baby pilot, and all around her she could see the things that had changed.

Most obvious was the yard where they were gathered. Sleepy Baby had grown, allowing Amy and Mark to finally move into a bigger house. They had waited longer than they probably needed, just to make sure they weren't taking unnecessary risks. But after more than a year of growth, and with a nice chunk of cash in the bank, they had finally bought this house, and moved in just a few weeks prior to Rick's going away party.

But it wasn't just about the place, it was about the people. Rick, the burgeoning entrepreneur, was chatting with Kevin about side businesses that he could run from a college dorm. Next to them, half listening and half watching Liam play in the grass, was Alyssa – who was very pregnant with their second child.

Mark and Daisy were barbecuing while David sat nearby and reminded them to flip the burgers before they burned. He rolled his cane back and forth on his knees – his rehab was progressing nicely, and it had been six months since he needed the wheelchair.

In fact, the recovery was going well enough that he no longer needed full-time help – maybe that's why Rosa was sitting with Amy's mastermind friends and chatting about business ideas!

Everything was exactly as Amy had hoped it would be, and it was all thanks to the online course that she had almost chickened out of launching on more than one occasion. There had continued to be bumps in the road of building and growing the business, but all in all things had progressed very nicely; she had learned a lot from the experience of helping her first cohort of students, and made some changes to the content of the course – explaining things better in places, trimming confusing bits in others, and adding a bonus module about self-care for parents that had been very well-received. After a second pilot run, Amy splurged for some nice video equipment, and created the "full" version of Sleepy Baby, which she was selling today.

Sales increased when Amy introduced a "refer a friend" option inside the course – it turns out that new parents tend to know other new parents. And sales picked up even more when she finally figured out how to sell the course with Facebook ads (her account was unfrozen after a lengthy appeals process). She had also negotiated a partnership with BabyHub, a major online portal for expectant parents, which had led to a great deal more sales. And she had just introduced a "concierge" level of her course, in which people could pay extra and have her take care of ordering all the gear that they needed.

As much as she appreciated the money and growth, though, Amy's favorite part was the stream of thank you notes from no-longer-sleep-deprived parents. That, more than anything, was what kept her motivated to keep growing the business.

Amy continued to meet with her friends in the mastermind group every two weeks, enjoying a new kind of cuisine each time. The group had been invaluable to her as she grew her business – both with moral support, and with concrete help and ideas (Devi wrote all of Amy's marketing copy, and the partnership with BabyHub had been Tamara's idea).

The others had grown a lot, too. Inspired by Amy's success, they had all taken a page from Amy's online course experience. Tamara had created a course that supplemented her consulting work – essentially recording herself explaining all the things that she would ordinarily have to explain to each and every client. The hybrid consulting-plus-course model meant that her trips could be a bit shorter, allowing her to actually attend more of the mastermind meetings. And, surprisingly to Tamara, the clients felt that consulting and a course was worth more than consulting alone, so she was able to raise her rates. Devi found a niche doing copywriting work for other course creators – enough to completely replace her cybersecurity job income, working less hours. In her free time, she had created a course on henna tattoo art, that had become wildly popular. And Tom had drawn from his decades in massage therapy to create a course showing people how to alleviate pain by changing the way they relate to their bodies. Tom wasn't looking to build an empire, so he just ran a live cohort of the program every few months to cover his bills while he worked on his book.

Amy was pulled from her reverie by Rick, who was calling to everyone. "Hey everyone, could you all listen up for a minute?"

They all quieted down, and all eyes turned to Rick.

"Since this is technically my going-away-to-college party, I wanted to say a few words." He said, looking uncomfortable but determined. "It's about my mom. A couple of years ago, I was pretty mad at her. We had moved out here from Ohio, away from my friends, and we were in this tiny apartment where I had to share a room with Daisy. And I knew that we didn't have a bigger place because mom was doing all these business things that didn't seem to go anywhere. I didn't really understand why she was doing it. All I knew was that if she had gotten a job, we'd have a bigger place and things would have been more comfortable. And I think that sometimes I was a little rude about it. I guess I was a dumb teenager."

"You're still a teenager." Daisy reminded him.

Rick glared at her, but continued. "You're right, but maybe I'm a little less dumb. Anyway, I didn't understand what my mom was doing, but now I do. She was building something that would make things a lot better. Like being able to live in this great house, that I'll enjoy for about a week before I move away. But it's not just about the house, or the money. I've been helping my mom with her website and sales systems, so I get to see the names and details of the people she's helping. And you guys, I don't know if you realize this – I don't even know if mom realizes this – but there was an important milestone for Sleepy Baby this week. We had our thousandth customer."

There was a smattering of applause.

"And it's not just about how many customers, or how many dollars that adds up to. Even though it's fun to do that math. But my favorite part is that those customers come from all over. We have customers in thirty-seven different states, in Canada, in Europe, and even in Australia. That's amazing. My mom built something that is helping people all over the world."

"Oh, Rick." Amy began to speak, but Rick interrupted her.

"Hang on, mom, I'm not finished." Rick thought for a moment, and then continued. "The thing is, my mom having something that she could teach isn't special. I mean, it is special, but in a way that a lot of people are special. She had something that she learned because she needed to, and because she was interested. Lots of people have something like that. And it was something that other people needed to know. What's really special about my mom is that she didn't take what she knew for granted. She realized that it was a gift, and that she could teach it to other people."

There was a long pause, and then Rick continued.

"Anyway, I feel like I've learned a lot from my mom over the last couple of years, and I'm really proud of her. I hope one day I can build something like she did."

The yard burst into applause, cheers, and well wishes as Amy gave her son a big, long hug.

TEACH YOUR GIFT

Hi there. It's Danny here – I'm the author. I hope you've enjoyed following Amy's story, and that you feel a little more inspired and empowered to pursue your own online course journey. I've also written a couple of books about online courses and marketing, that I hope will support you in deepening your understanding of these areas, and seizing the opportunities that they represent. I'd like to gift you a copy of both of those books, and you'll find instructions on how to claim them in just a few pages. But first, to whet your appetite, what follows is the opening of my non-fiction book about online course businesses, called Teach Your Gift. *I hope you love it!*

My heart pounded and my fingers trembled as my eyes darted across my online banking statement. My accounts were all empty, and my credit cards were maxed out.

I felt shell-shocked. My start-up company had crumbled, and my last employee was gone. What was I going to do? Circumstances had left me with over a quarter of a million dollars of debt, and my consulting practice had completely dried up. I had no money, no income, and no prospects... only debt. How did I get here?

I wanted to make the world a better place, and I thought I'd do it with a start-up company. We built educational software to help kids learn how to read. I bootstrapped the company through prototypes, proof of concept, a product launch, and market testing. The product was great—kids loved it, and so did the experts in the field. But I was young and inexperienced, and I made a mistake. Parents and teachers—our actual customers—didn't get it. We were bleeding money but managed to pivot the product to an educational virtual world for kids. Feedback was spectacular, and all we needed was money to make it happen. I spent every penny I had to keep it going long enough for an investor to write us a check, and just as we were getting tantalizingly close... the market crash of 2008 hit. Game over. I was so far in the red that I forgot there were other colors. I had to let my employees go, and wind down the company. Meanwhile, I had been so busy with my start-up that my consulting business had been neglected, and the pipeline was dry.

I did what anyone would do when left with no alternative: I started over. I parlayed my hard- and expensive-won expertise into a new consulting business and hit the networking circuit. I took every meeting and pursued every opportunity. And by the time a few years had passed, I was doing all right. Sure, some months were more comfortable than others, but the pain of failure was no longer so acute. I was fine.

Except that I wasn't fine. Sure, I was earning decent money, but I was also carrying so much debt that I expected to spend most of my adult life paying it off. And I wasn't exactly in love with every client I had to chase (or with the actual chasing!). But it wasn't just about money or lifestyle. I had the same nagging feeling that afflicts so many of the coaches, consultants, authors, and speakers I've met over the last decade: the feeling that I could be making more of an impact than I was. That the skills, expertise, and insights I'd spent a lifetime developing could help more than the people I happened to meet at local networking mixers.

So I started writing. I was inspired by the emerging zeitgeist of blogging and social media, and the promise that through the internet one might touch the lives of millions. I poured my heart (and my best ideas) onto the proverbial page, and agonized to make every word perfect. There was just one problem: Nobody actually read any of it. I discovered what every burgeoning online entrepreneur learns sooner or later: that creating something great is only a small piece of the puzzle of building an actual business.

I tried to learn what was missing; I read every article and book that I could get my hands on. Much of it was out of date, and even the best stuff was able to help me understand only *what* to do, not *how* to do it. I looked for experts who might be able to help, but few people seemed to have the skills I really needed, and those who did were far beyond my budget and risk tolerance. I felt stuck and stymied. Thankfully, things were about to look up.

In all my internet browsing, I stumbled across an on-line course being offered by a blogger, who has since become a trusted friend. He had the exact expertise I needed, and while I couldn't afford to hire him as a personal advisor, I could spring for his online course. And thank goodness that I did, because that's the first time that online courses changed my life. By applying his ideas, and then building on them with my own, I was finally able to get eyes on my work, and word began to spread. I was even starting to attract consulting clients through the internet—something that had never happened before.

Then something surprising happened. All those people who followed my work and watched my slow climb to become a D-level internet celebrity started reaching out to me with questions and requests. They wanted me to do more than just write articles—they wanted me to create an online course of my own, teaching some of the strategies that I had developed. It took some time for me to warm up to the idea, but eventually I gave it a shot. That was the second time that online courses changed my life. My small team and I were blown away by the demand; that single online course led to another, and then another. My business grew: in just a few years we went from a one-person consultancy to a team of several dozen people, serving thousands of students through our courses and coaching programs.

I feel lucky to have discovered the world of online courses early, before it was cool. But these days, the cat is clearly out of the bag. Online courses have come a long way from their obscurity just a few years ago. Today everyone is getting in on the action—from pop stars to celebrity chefs, from relationship experts to business gurus, from athletes to authors, and everyone in between. You can get their courses from publishers like MasterClass and CreativeLive, through marketplaces like Udemy and LinkedIn Learning, and of course on the websites of hundreds of thousands of independent course creators who avail themselves of self-serve platforms like Thinkific, Teachable, and Ruzuku—all driving the rapid growth of an industry already valued at multiple hundreds of billions of dollars, as reported by TJ McCue on Forbes.

In fact, online courses have become so ubiquitous that it's easy to forget how new of a phenomenon they really are. Even a few years ago, to receive instruction from the leading experts in your field was a fantasy – unless you could afford astronomical consulting rates, or were one of the privileged few that luck or circumstance had placed in direct contact with them. But the emergence and evolution of a host of technologies has made possible the holy grail for people seeking to create impact by (and profit from) sharing their expertise: leverage.

Of course, leverage isn't a new idea. It was in the third century BCE that the Greek mathematician Archimedes famously said that with a lever long enough and a fulcrum on which to place it, he could move the world. It's a powerful idea, fundamentally about being smart with the resources that you have in order to get the most bang for your buck.

That's what engineers do with physical levers and fulcrums, but it's also the concept that real estate developers use to buy much more land than the cash in their pockets is worth and that political operatives use when they trade favors in pursuit of their agendas. In all cases, they place their resources (a physical lever, the cash and credibility they've earned, or a juicy piece of gossip) where they'll get the most bang for their buck (a fulcrum, a lending institution, or a gossip columnist).

Experts aren't new to the application of leverage either, but for most of human history we were limited by the technology of the day. Yes, you know what I'm talking about—you're holding it in your hand right now. For most of human history, the primary vehicle of knowledge transfer was the book. And books are great for a lot of things; as a reader, I'm grateful to the countless authors who've opened my mind, expanded my horizons, and planted seeds in my imagination. And as a writer, I'm (grudgingly) appreciative of how the writing process forces us to refine and clarify our thinking.

But while books are great for transmitting ideas, sharing perspectives, and adding new knowledge to existing expertise, they're not very good at imparting competence or capability. Put simply, people don't usually develop skills or get good at doing things by reading about them—that takes a more involved intervention, which includes opportunities for practice combined with the interactivity and dynamism of meaningful and timely feedback. The way to do that for most of history has been to work closely with a teacher; whether through lectures and assignments, explicit apprenticeships, or the implicit pact between employer and employee to "learn on the job," you had to be in fairly close contact with your instructor.

But gradually over the past couple of decades, technology made possible an ever-richer learning experience that could deliver real competence and transformation to the dedicated student. And that was the gateway to real leverage.

All of a sudden, experts could meaningfully impart the transformation that their skills provide to as many students who wanted to learn and benefit. The sky was the limit, as evidenced by the throngs of learners who rushed to embrace the opportunities that they heretofore couldn't afford or access. And that excitement was music to the ears of all those intrepid course creators, who could suddenly reach far more people (and earn far more income). And it's not just about the reach or income either—the best part of it all for course entrepreneurs is the freedom:

Financial freedom, for one. This isn't the only thing, but it's definitely important. Leverage means that you're no longer constrained by the direct trade of hours for dollars. I'm certainly grateful to earn a comfortable living and to have been able to pay my debts. This potential for financial return is what attracts many course creators to this opportunity.

The freedom to choose your own hours. Since you aren't directly beholden to any individual student, you don't have a clock to punch, so you can choose both how much to work and what schedule best suits you, your family, and your priorities.

The freedom to travel. This can mean taking dream vacations, going on extended trips, spending months at a time in new destinations, or living the life of a digital nomad since just about everything that course businesses involve can be done from anywhere with a stable internet connection, and entrepreneurs aren't beholden to employers who count vacation days.

The freedom NOT to travel. Whereas many course entrepreneurs are excited to travel more, there are also a lot of frequent fliers who are tired of getting on planes that take them away from their lives and families on a weekly basis. The ability to serve through an online course can change business travel from a necessity to a choice. This freedom in particular has become especially important in the post-COVID-19 era of working from home!

The freedom to do stuff that matters. This is the most important freedom of all, whether it means spending more time with your kids, scaling the impact of your expertise, or dedicating your energies to the causes that you care about.

No wonder so many experts are flocking to join the online course revolution, drawn to this alluring cocktail of leverage, freedom, and impact. I know, because I've had the privilege of being in the eye of the online courses tornado for most of the last decade. Since I got involved in this world, I've written about online courses for major publications, spoken about them at conferences and to organizations, and published multiple books as the landscape has evolved.

And while I take an academic interest in understanding what makes the world of online courses tick, I've also had the practical experience of working with thousands of online course creators that were trained through my company's online training programs (yes, courses about courses... it's very meta, I know!).

Over the years, I've encountered thousands of consultants, coaches, speakers, authors, and experts who are excited by the idea of what an online course can do for their businesses and lives, but aren't quite clear on what it will take to go from a good idea to a thriving course business. Or worse, they think they know, but they're working off of a playbook that's woefully out of date. Remember, we're talking about internet years here, and things have changed a lot! To set the record straight, and give a working blueprint that can be followed by those experts (of which I assume you are one), I wrote this book—may it support you on your journey to teach your gift.

My goal in this book is to show you the blueprint for online course business success that works today and into the future—one that you can use to create the leverage, freedom, and impact that you know courses can add to your business and life. We'll do this through five chapters:

A Brief History of Online Courses. We'll start with a quick review of the history of online courses. You'll learn how things came to be the way they are today, and understand the nuances of the landscape from which you'll launch your online course business.

Your Course and Your Business. Next we'll talk about the different ways that an online course can fit into a business, and you'll decide which configuration makes the most sense for you and for your students. Getting this right is the real key to the leverage, freedom, and impact that attracts people to the world of online courses in the first place.

From Good Idea to Winning Course. Here you'll learn the actual course creation blueprint: what to do first, second, and third as you turn your idea into a course, and what potholes to avoid along the way – including some of the most powerful techniques that we teach students in our online course creation training programs.

How to Attract Paying Students. These are the sixty-four-million-dollar questions on every course builder's mind: Where do I find paying students, and how do I enroll them in my courses? The answers will vary based on the stage of the course business journey that you're on, and we'll explore the best answer for you so that you can get the results that you're looking for.

Creating a World-Class Course. Finally, we'll do a deep dive into what's on the cutting edge of online course creation today so that you can both stay current and get ahead of the competition to create a course that delivers transformation and engenders testimonials, referrals, and repeat business from your students.

I hope you've enjoyed this excerpt. I've done my very best to pour the very best of my expertise into Teach Your Gift, *and I'm honored to offer you a free copy of that book, as well as my companion book about online business and marketing called* Effortless. *To access free copies of both, follow the links that you'll find on the next page. Good luck!*

Bonus resources to support you!

GET THE ONLINE COURSE BUSINESS BUNDLE (FREE)

The audiobook version of this book (narrated by a team of actors!) PLUS the audio versions of two other books I've written about online course businesses: Teach Your Gift, and Effortless..

→ Download it at **OnlineCourses.Rocks/bundle**

PARTICIPATE IN THE COURSE BUILDER'S BOOTCAMP (FREE)

Ready to start your own online course business journey? Our weeklong intensive Course Builder's Bootcamp is a crash course in everything you need to get started.

→ Sign up for free at **OnlineCourses.Rocks/bootcamp**

JOIN US IN PERSON AT TEACH YOUR GIFT LIVE

Receive best-in-class training, discover cutting-edge strategies, and connect with a community of your fellow coach, consultant, author, speaker, and expert entrepreneurs.

→ Reserve your spot at **OnlineCourses.Rocks/live**

ACKNOWLEDGEMENTS

The more books I write, the more I appreciate that book writing is a team sport. Without many great people around me, I wouldn't have the knowledge or experience about which to write, the time or focus to put proverbial pen to paper, or even the logistical support to turn my typo-riddled manuscript into the near-pristine work that you hold in your hand. So yes, there are a lot of people to thank!

Topping the list are the wonderful people that I get to work with every day at Mirasee, where we teach coaches, consultants, authors, speakers and experts to teach their gift and grow their businesses – and of course the students that we have the privilege of working with, supporting, and also learning from. They're the real Amys.

Special thanks go to Sean Platt and his team at Sterling & Stone, who helped me craft a narrative arc to carry my ideas. If you found the story engaging, Sean and his team deserve a lot of the credit.

Deep gratitude also to Ally Machate and the entire publishing team behind her at The Writer's Ally. Thank you for making the book in my hands better than I imagined it would be in my mind.

And most of all, my family. Bhoomi, you are my partner at home, and my partner at work. I hit the marriage jackpot, and tempted as I sometimes am to take that for granted, I will do my best to always remember how lucky I am. Priya and Micah, I'm so proud of you both – your poise, your curiosity, your initiative, and everything else that makes you both so wonderful. It is my privilege to watch you grow, and to learn so much from you both.

ABOUT THE AUTHOR

Danny Iny is the founder and CEO of the online business education company Mirasee, whose work on strategy training won special recognition from *Fast Company* as a "World Changing Idea." He has been featured in the *Harvard Business Review* and *Entrepreneur*, and contributes regularly to publications including *Inc.*, *Forbes*, and *Business Insider*. He has spoken at institutions like Yale University and organizations like Google, and is the author of multiple books about online courses and business, including two editions of *Teach and Grow Rich* (in 2015 and 2017), *Leveraged Learning* (in 2018), *Teach Your Gift* (in 2020), and *Effortless* (in 2021). He lives in Montreal, Canada with his wife Bhoomi (who is his partner in both life and business), and their children Priya and Micah.